THE "K. H." LETTERS

TO

C. W. LEADBEATER

WITH A COMMENTARY BY

C. JINARAJADASA

1980

THE THEOSOPHICAL PUBLISHING HOUSE

ADYAR, MADRAS, INDIA

68, Great Russell Street, London, WCIB 3BU England.
Post Box 270, Wheaton, Illinois 60187, U.S.A.

First Edition *1941*
Reprinted *1980*

C. W. LEADBEATER
in 1883

C. W. LEADBEATER
in 1931

CONTENTS

THE "K. H." LETTERS TO C. W. LEADBEATER

On November 21, 1883, C. W. Leadbeater signed his application form to join the Theosophical Society ; on March 1, 1934, he passed out of incarnation. The sole interest of his life during fifty-one years was to work for the Society ; he has to his credit a magnificent record of service rendered to mankind through his lectures on Theosophy in many lands, and through his books on many aspects of the Ancient Wisdom. What was the driving power in his life which made him firm and faithful to the end ?

That driving power came from the fact that *he found his Master* in October, 1884. For it was then that he was accepted as a " chela " or disciple by the Adept who called himself Koot Hoomi, and signed his communications with the two initials K. H. How Mr. Leadbeater came to receive certain letters from the Master K. H., and what were his reactions to them, must be examined, if we are to understand him and his life's work.

The first chapter in any biography of C. W. Leadbeater must begin with this incident. For when the significance of that incident is grasped, and when his action at the time is rightly appraised, then we can see why opportunity after opportunity came to him of service, and why thousands in many lands—men and women, boys and girls—looked to him as to a father, brother and friend, for guidance and inspiration.

In 1883, Mr. Leadbeater was a clergyman of the Church of England, and was acting as curate in the Parish of Bramshott, Hampshire, England. He had for many years been deeply interested in Spiritualism, not in the inspirational addresses of the spirits through their mediums, but in the phenomena performed by those spirits which revealed not only the existence of unsuspected powers in nature but also the command over them by discarnate entities. I will let Mr. Leadbeater now take up the story.

Mr. William Eglinton

" In the course of my inquiries into Spiritualism I had come into contact with most of the prominent mediums of that day, and had seen every one of the ordinary phenomena about which one reads in books upon that subject. One medium with whom I had much to do was Mr. Eglinton ; and although I have heard stories told against him, I must bear witness that in all my own dealings with him I found him most straightforward, reasonable and courteous. He had various so-called controls—one a Red Indian girl who called herself Daisy, and chattered volubly on all occasions, appropriate or inappropriate. Another was a tall Arab, named Abdallah, considerably over six feet, who never said anything, but produced remarkable phenomena, and often exhibited feats showing great strength. I have seen him simultaneously lift two heavy men, one in each hand.

" A third control who frequently put in an appearance was Ernest ; he comparatively rarely materialized, but frequently spoke with direct voice, and wrote a characteristic and well-educated hand. One day in conversation with him something was said in reference to the Masters of the Wisdom ; Ernest spoke of Them with the most profound reverence, and said that he had on various occasions had the privilege of seeing Them. I at once enquired whether he was prepared to take charge of any message or letter for Them, and he said that he would willingly do so, and would deliver it when opportunity offered, but he could not say exactly when that would be.

" To return to my story, I at once provisionally accepted Ernest's offer. I said that I would write a letter to one of these Great Masters, and would confide it to him if my friend and teacher, Mr. Sinnett, approved. At the mention of this name the " spirits " were much perturbed ; Daisy especially was very angry, and declared that she would have nothing to do with Mr. Sinnett under any circumstances ;

" Why, he calls us spooks ! ", she said, with great indignation. However, I blandly stuck to my point that all I knew of Theosophy had come to me through Mr. Sinnett, and that I therefore did not feel justified in going behind his back in any way, or trying to find some other means of communication without first consulting him. Finally, though with a very bad grace, the spirits consented to this, and the séance presently terminated. When Mr. Eglinton came out of his trance, I asked him how I could send a letter to Ernest, and he said at once that if I would let him have the letter he would put it in a certain box which hung against the wall, from which Ernest would take it when he wished. I then posted off to Mr. Sinnett, and asked his opinion of all this. He was at once eagerly interested, and advised me promptly to accept the offer and see what happened.

A letter to the Master

" Thereupon I went home and wrote three letters. The first was to the Master K. H., telling Him with all reverence that ever since I had first heard of Theosophy my one desire had been to place myself under Him as a pupil. I told Him of my circumstances at the time, and asked whether it was necessary that the seven years of probation of which I had heard should be passed in India. I put this letter in a small envelope and sealed it carefully with my own seal. Then I enclosed it in a letter to Ernest in which I reminded him of his promise, and asked him to deliver this letter for me, and to bring back an answer if there should be one. That second letter I sealed in the same manner as the first, and then I enclosed that in turn with a short note to Eglinton, asking him to put it in his box, and let me know whether any notice was taken of it. I had asked a friend who was staying with me to examine the seals of both the letters with a microscope, so that if we should see them again we might know whether any one had been tampering with them. By return of post I received a note from Mr. Eglinton, saying that he had duly put the note for Ernest into his box, and that it had already vanished, and further that if any reply should come to him he would at once forward it.

" A few days later I received a letter directed in a hand which was unknown to me, and on opening it I discovered my own letter to Ernest apparently unopened, the name 'Ernest' on the envelope being crossed out, and my own written underneath it in pencil. My friend and I once more examined the seal with a microscope, and were unable to to detect any indication whatever that any one had tampered with the letter, and we both agreed that it was quite impossible that it could have been opened ; yet on cutting it open I discovered that the letter which I had written to the Master had disappeared. All that I found inside was my own letter to Ernest, with a few words in the well-known hand-writing of the latter written on its blank page, to the effect that my letter had been duly handed to the Great Master, and that if in the future I should ever be thought worthy to receive an answer Ernest would gladly bring it to me.

" I waited for some months, but no reply came, and whenever I went to Eglinton's séances and happened to encounter Ernest, I always asked him when I might expect my answer. He invariably said that my letter had been duly delivered, but that nothing had yet been said about an answer, and that he could do no more." [1]

The letter referred to above was sent to the Master K. H. on March 3, 1884. On November 1st of that year, Madame Blavatsky was to sail for India with Mr. and Mrs. A. J. Cooper-Oakley. Two days before, on October 30th, Mr. Leadbeater came to London to say good-bye to H. P. B., and stayed the night with Mr. and Mrs. A. P. Sinnett. That evening he was informed by " D. K." (the Master Djual Khool), through H. P. B., that a reply to his letter of March 3rd had been sent by the Master, but nothing was said as to its contents.

[1] *How Theosophy came to me*, pp. 29-35.

On the morning of October 31st, Mr. Leadbeater returned to Liphook (the station for Bramshott parish) by the 11. 35 train from Waterloo Station. As Liphook is forty-seven miles from London, he would have arrived at Bramshott about one o'clock. There he found the letter, whose exact reproduction I give.[1]

---

[1] This letter is in blue-pencil handwriting. It is not written with the hand but "precipitated," a process which requires the use of occult powers. The Master K. H. describes the process as follows in two letters to Mr. A. P. Sinnett :

"Bear in mind that these my letters are not written but *impressed* or precipitated, and then mistakes corrected ".

"For, whether I ' precipitate' or dictate them or write my answers myself, the difference in time saved is very minute. I have to *think* it over, to photograph every word and sentence carefully in my brain, before it can be repeated by ' precipitation '. As the fixing on chemically prepared surfaces of the images formed by the camera requires a previous arrangement within the focus of the object to be represented, for otherwise—as often found in bad photographs—the legs of the sitter might appear out of all proportion with the head, and so on ; so we have to arrange our sentences, and impress every letter to appear on paper, in our minds before it becomes fit to be read. For the present that is *all* I can tell you. When science will have learned more about the mystery of the *lithophyl* (or lithobiblion) and how the impress of leaves comes originally to take place on stones, then I will be able to make you better understand the process." (*The Mahatma Letters to A. P. Sinnett*, pp. 19, 22.)

There is a second description of precipitation in a letter of H. P. B. to Mr. Sinnett. After mentioning that a precipitated letter will show on an examination by a microscope " several layers of various stuffs—black lead, and powder and ink, etc.", H.P.B. describes how she has observed her own Master, the Master M., at the work of precipitating.

"I have often seen M. sit with a book of most elaborate Chinese characters that he wanted to copy, and a blank book before him, and then rub it in slightly on the page ; and then over it precipitate ink ; and then, if the image of the characters was all right and correct in his mind, the characters copied would be all right, and if he happened to be interrupted, then there would be a blunder and the work would be spoilt." (*The Letters of H. P. Blavatsky to A. P. Sinnett*, p. 32.)

Last spring — March the 3d
you wrote a letter to me & entrusted it to "Ernest." Tho' the
paper itself never reached
me — nor was it ever likely
to, considering the nature of the
messenger — its contents have.
I did not answer it at the
time but sent you a warning
thro' upasika.

In that message of yours it
was said that, since reading
Esot. Bud: & Isis your "one
great wish has been to place
yourself under me as a chela
that you may learn more of
the truth." "I understand
from Mr S." you went on
"that it would be almost impossible to become a chela without going out to India"

You hoped to be able to do that in a few years, tho' for the present ties of gratitude bind you to remain in this country. Etc.

I now answer the above & your other questions.

[1] IT is not necessary that one should be in India during the seven years of probation. A chela can pass them anywhere.

[2] To accept any man as a chela does not depend on my personal will. It can be only the result of one's personal merit and exertions in that direction. Force any one of the "masters" you may happen to choose; do good works in his name & for the love of mankind; be pure & resolute in the path of righteousness [as laid out in our rules]; be honest & unselfish; forget your Self but to remember the

good of other people — and you will have forced that "master" to accept you.

So much for candidates during the periods of the undisturbed progress of your Society. There is something more to be done, however, when theosophy — the Cause of Truth, is, as at the present moment on its stand for life or death before the tribunal of Public opinion — that most flippantly cruel, prejudiced & unjust of all tribunals. There is also the collective Karma of the caste you belong to — to be considered. It is undeniable that the Cause you have at heart is now suffering owing to the dark intrigues, the base conspiracy of the Christian clergy and missionaries against the Society. They will

Stop before writing to ruin the reputation of the Founders. Are you willing to atone for their Sins? Then go to Adyar for a few months. "The ties of gratitude" will not be severed, nor even become weakened for an absence of a few months if the step be explained plainly to your relative. He who would shorten the years of probation has to make sacrifices for theosophy. Pushed by malevolent hands to the very edge of a precipice, the Society needs every man and woman Strong in the cause of truth. It is by doing noble actions & not by only determining that they shall be done that the fruits of the meritorious actions are reaped. Like the "true man" of Carlyle who is not to be seduced by Ease

(2

—"difficulty, abnegation, martyrdom, death are the allurements
that act during the hours of
trial on the heart of a true chela.
    You ask me —"what rules I
must observe during this time
of probation & how soon I might
venture to hope that it could begin". I answer: You have the
making of your own future,
in your own hands as I shown
above, and Every day you may
be weaving its woof. If I were
to demand that you should do
one thing or the other, instead of
simply advising, I would be
responsible for every Effect that
might flow from the Step, & you
acquire but a Secondary merit.
I think, & you will see that this is
true. So cast the lot yourself
into the lap of Justice, never

fearing but that its response will be absolutely true. Chelaship is an educational as well as probationary stage & the chela alone can determine whether it shall end in adeptship or failure. Chelas from a mistaken idea of our system too often watch & wait for orders, wasting precious time which should be taken up with personal effort. Our cause needs missionaries, devotees, agents, even martyrs perhaps. But it cannot demand of any man to make himself either. So now choose & grasp your own destiny — and may our Lord's the Tathâgata's memory aid you to decide for the best.

K H.

FIRST LETTER FROM THE MASTER K. H.

Last spring—March the 3rd—you wrote a letter to me and entrusted it to "Ernest". Tho' the paper itself never reached me—nor was it ever likely to, considering the nature of the messenger—its contents have. I did not answer it at the time, but sent you a warning through Upasika.

In that message of yours it was said that, since reading Esot. Bud: and Isis your "one great wish has been to place yourself under me as a chela, that you may learn more of the truth." "I understand from Mr. S." you went on "that it would be almost impossible to become a chela without going out to India". You hoped to be able to do that in a few years, tho' for the present ties of gratitude bind you to remain in this country. Etc.

I now answer the above and your other questions.

(1) It is not necessary that one should be in India during the seven years of probation. A chela can pass them anywhere.

(2) To accept any man as a chela does not depend on my personal will. It can only be the result of one's personal merit and exertions in that direction. Force any one of the "Masters" you may happen to choose; do good works in his name and for the love of mankind; be pure and resolute in the path of righteousness (as laid out in our rules); be honest and unselfish; forget your Self but to remember the good of other people—and you will have forced that "Master" to accept you.

So much for candidates during the periods of the undisturbed progress of your Society. There is something more to be done, however, when theosophy, the Cause of

Truth, is, as at the present moment on its stand for life or death before the tribunal of public opinion—that most flippantly cruel, prejudiced and unjust of all tribunals. There is also the collective karma of the caste you belong to, to be considered. It is undeniable that the cause you have at heart is now suffering owing to the dark intrigues, the base conspiracy of the Christian clergy and missionaries against the Society. They will stop before nothing to ruin the reputation of the Founders. Are you willing to atone for their sins? Then go to Adyar for a few months. " The ties or gratitude " will not be severed, nor even become weakened for an absence of a few months if the step be explained plausibly to your relative. He who would shorten the years of probation has to make sacrifices for theosophy. Pushed by malevolent hands to the very edge of a precipice, the Society needs every man and woman strong in the cause of truth. It is by doing noble actions and not by only determining that they shall be done that the fruits of the meritorious actions are reaped. Like the " true man " of Carlyle who is not to be seduced by ease, " difficulty, abnegation, martyrdom, death are the allurements that act " during the hours of trial on the heart of a true chela.

You ask me, " what rules I must observe during this time of probation, and how soon I might venture to hope that it could begin ". I answer : you have the making of your own future, in your own hands as shown above, and every day you may be weaving its woof. If I were to demand that you should do one thing or the other, instead of simply advising, I would be responsible for every effect that might flow from the step and you acquire but a secondary merit. Think, and you will see that this is true. So cast the lot yourself into the lap of Justice, never fearing but that its response will be absolutely true. Chelaship is an educational as well as probationary stage and the chela alone can determine whether it shall end in adeptship or failure. Chelas from a mistaken idea of our system too often watch and wait for orders, wasting precious time which should be taken up with personal effort. Our cause needs missionaries, devotees, agents, even martyrs perhaps. But it cannot demand of any man to make himself either. So now choose and grasp your own destiny, and may our Lord's the Tathâgata's memory aid you to decide for the best.

K. H.

COMMENTARY

As this letter of the Master is full of illumination to students of Occultism, I propose, after the manner of the commentators of old of the Vedas and the Upanishads, to comment on all phrases in it which require elucidation, in order to bring out the full significance of the Master's thought.

Last Spring, March 3rd

As already mentioned, it was on March 3, 1884, that Mr. Leadbeater wrote the letter to the Master. He dispatched it to "Ernest", the spirit, in the manner which has been described by him already.

entrusted it to "Ernest"

The chief spirit "control" of the mediums was John King, who claimed to be Sir Henry Morgan, the English buccaneer who sacked the city of Panama in 1671. In some ways, John King was the "boss" of the spirits and kept them in order. But "Ernest" never revealed who he had been when incarnate.

considering the nature of the messenger

Ernest was mistaken when he thought that he could enter the presence of the Adepts, even to deliver a letter, unless permitted by them to do so. But it looks as if Ernest was merely bluffing, and trying to be amiable to Mr. Leadbeater, when he promised to deliver the letter. Mr. Leadbeater comments on this as follows :

> "I may mention here that in connection with this I had later a good example of the unreliability of all such communications. Some considerable time afterwards some spiritualist wrote to *Light* explaining that there could not

possibly be such persons as the Masters, because Ernest had positively told him that there were not. I wrote to the same newspaper to say that I had it on precisely the same valueless authority that there were *Masters*, and that Ernest knew them well. In each case Ernest had evidently reflected the thought of the questioner, as such entities so often do."[1]

its contents have

Years afterwards, when Mr. Leadbeater was able through the unfolding of his psychic powers to communicate directly with the Master, without the aid of any intermediary, the Master informed him that as he (C.W.L.) was writing the letter at his home at Bramshott, then and there the Master had read the letter. Therefore though Ernest never delivered the letter, and it never reached the Master, " its contents have."

sent you a warning thro' Upasika

The word Upâsikâ is the feminine of the Pâli word Upâsaka. An Upâsaka is a man who takes the " eight vows ", and an Upâsikâ a woman who takes the same vows. (A Buddhist monk takes two more vows in addition). The nearest Western rendering of the word is Lay Brother and Lay Sister. Upâsikâ is the word often used by the Masters for H.P.B., as during her period of residence with them in Tibet she had taken the vows of a Lay Sister. The warning referred to was an intimation by H.P.B. to Mr. Leadbeater to moderate his enthusiasm for spiritualistic phenomena ; but she did not mention then that the warning was from the Master. Hence Mr. Leadbeater did not know at the time that the Master was aware of his offer of service and dedication.

ties of gratitude bind you

Mr. Leadbeater was at this time one of two curates or assistant priests of the Church of England, in the parish of Bramshott,

[1] *How Theosophy came to me*, p. 31.

Liphook, Hampshire. The Rector or priest-in-charge was the Rev. W. W. Capes, who was also Rural Dean. Mr. Capes was the uncle of Mr. Leadbeater and an Oxford " don ", being the Reader in Ancient History in the University, Fellow of Queen's College, and for some time tutor of Hertford College. Mr. Leadbeater's father had died some years before, and he was the only surviving son; his mother and he were well-to-do, when the Leadbeater family lost all in the collapse of a great bank. This necessitated his going to work as early as possible; for a while he was a clerk in the well-known bank of Williams Deacons & Co. But the work was naturally cramping and uncongenial. He was very " High Church " in his ecclesiastic leanings, and was closely associated with the work of the Church of All Saints, Margaret Street, London. As his uncle had much influence in ecclesiastic circles, it seemed logical that the nephew should enter the Church. After the usual studies he was admitted as Deacon by Bishop Harold Browne of Winchester on December 22, 1878, and ordained Priest on December 21, 1879, at the Parish Church of St. Andrew, Farnham, Surrey. When admitted as Deacon, he was authorized to act as a curate at Bramshott, a very large parish. During term time, the Rector, the Rev. Mr. Capes, was often away at Oxford on his University work, and the routine work of the large parish fell largely upon the two curates. Mr. Leadbeater therefore felt that he could scarcely leave for India without creating difficulties for his uncle, to whom he owed much, to find a substitute.

one should be in India

Since the Theosophical Movement was originated by two Adepts who live in Indian bodies, and since a large number of Adepts are similarly in Eastern bodies, there was naturally an idea among the early Theosophists that there was no possibility of real spiritual growth and occult advancement unless one went to India. This idea still prevails among those who in Europe and the Americas believe in the existence of the Masters. There are hundreds in those lands who think that there can be no beginning of any spiritual advancement, unless they make every effort to free themselves from

2

their Western environment, and come to India in search of a Master.

It is only after one realizes the true nature of the Adept, and how his consciousness can function in an instant in any part of the world, and how his mind responds instantaneously wherever the sincere thought of an aspirant flashes out in the invisible, that one knows that it is not necessary to leave one's place of residence, in order to come close to a Master. All of us who are " sons of the Master " know by personal experience how he is aware of every thought and feeling of ours, wherever we may be, and how he gives his directions for important actions in his service. Of several instances which show how the Adept *knows*, though he may be thousands of miles away, I select two.

In the year 1884, one of the most devoted members of the Theosophical Society was Miss Francesca Arundale. She received in London a long letter from the Master K. H.[1], at the time in Tibet, from which I quote three extracts :

(1) " I have followed your many thoughts. I have watched their silent evolution and the yearnings of your inner soul ; and since your pledge permits me to do so, having a few things to tell you concerning yourself and those you love, I take the opportunity . . . to write to you directly to say a few words."

(2) " Having overheard your conversation with H. P. B. on the night of her arrival, I may say that you are right."

(3) " She [Miss Arundale's mother] is unconsciously doing herself harm, great harm, by not curbing her temper. She draws to herself bad ' astral ' influences and creates a current so antagonistic to ours that we are often forced sorrowfully away."

The second instance of the Adept knowing at once what is happening thousands of miles away, relates to Colonel H. S. Olcott. In 1888 when he was proceeding to London to meet H. P. B., he was on board a steamer which was approaching Brindisi. On the early morning of the day before the arrival, when on deck, he felt irritated against H. P. B., thinking that her then policy in Europe

---

[1] Published in *Letters from the Masters of the Wisdom*, First Series, Letter No. XX.

would make a division in the Society. When he returned to his cabin, there dropped from the air a long letter from the Master K. H. full of advice and instruction, regarding the situation which he would find in London.[1] In that letter appear these sentences.

> "One of the most valuable effects of Upasika's mission is that it drives men to self-study and destroys in them blind servility for persons. Observe your own case, for example. But your revolt, good friend, against her 'infallibility'—as you once thought it—has gone too far, and you have been unjust to her, for which, I am sorry to say, you will have to suffer hereafter, along with others. Just now, on deck, your thoughts about her were dark and sinful, and so I find the moment a fitting one to put you on your guard."

We see thus that distance makes no difference to an Adept, and that though he may be thousands of miles away, his attention is immediately drawn to anyone who sincerely and profoundly aspires, or to any one of his pupils as he does his Master's work. It has been said by one of the Masters that, in the world today, where there are so few who unselfishly desire to serve mankind, or yearn for true spirituality, wherever an earnest soul seeks the Light, it is as if in an utterly dark valley a man were to light a candle. The candle may be small, but so great is the surrounding darkness, that its light is seen far away. In a similar manner, the man who seeks, purely, unselfishly, strenuously, to come to the Light is known at once by the Masters, in whatever part of the world that man may abide. And to the measure of his aspiration and his capability for receiving the Light of Wisdom, that Light is given to him. Hence, " It is not necessary that one should be in India during the seven years of probation. A *chela* can pass them anywhere."

does not depend on my personal will.

Here for the first time we find an idea which is quite the reverse of what has been the usual conception, regarding the acceptance of a pupil by an occult teacher. In India the idea has been prevalent as an immemorial tradition that the would-be-disciple had

[1] *Letters from the Masters of the Wisdom,* First Series, Letter No. XIX.

only to go to a Guru and say, " Sir, accept me ", and the Guru would
reply, " So be it ". It is true that, in one of the Upanishads, a teacher
replies to the candidate, " Return after one year ", and that this reply
is given a second time, at the end of the first year.

A revealing idea is presented by the Master K. H. that in
Occultism the relation between Master and pupil is not a sentimental
one ; it has to be the result of the setting in motion of definite forces by
the would-be-disciple. This idea is conveyed in the words that the
relation can only be established as " the result of one's personal merit
and exertions in that direction ".   It is only after much knowledge of
what is the work of an Adept that one realizes that a Master is not
just a mere teacher of spiritual truths, but is essentially a great executive
agent who handles the forces of the Logos, and as such is responsible
for even their slightest use.   The relation between Master and pupil
implies that the Master must utilize some of those forces, which are in
his charge, to help the pupil. He must therefore have proof that it
will be worth his while to divert those forces towards the pupil,
and that the pupil will return back to the Master's reservoir of force
more than he has received from it.

Force any one of the " Masters "

Nothing could be more striking than the use of the word
" *force* ", and underlining it, so as to draw special attention to the
reality behind the thought.   There is the occult saying, " Knock and
it shall be opened unto you "; but it does not follow, as has
been explained in *Light on the Path*, that a mere desire on the
part of an aspirant is a real " knock ", in the occult significance of
the word.

> " Those that ask shall have.   But though the ordinary man
> asks perpetually, his voice is not heard.   For he asks
> with his mind only ; and the voice of the mind is only
> heard on that plane on which the mind acts." (*Light on
> the Path.*)

The aspirant must so determine the direction of all his thoughts
and feelings that they converge on the hope of being received as a
pupil.   If such a determination is carried out *in action*, day after **day,**

it may be for years sometimes, he "knocks" at the door of the Master, and the Master as an agent of the Great Law must open the door, for the aspirant will have "*forced* that ' Master ' ".

the " Masters "

It is noteworthy that the Master K. H. in the letter twice puts the word "Master" between inverted commas. So similarly, in a letter to Miss F. Arundale, written a few months before this to Mr. Leadbeater, the Master writes "Masters" when referring to the Adepts. This is noteworthy as drawing attention to the fact that the Adepts have never called themselves "Masters" but simply "Brothers". Naturally enough, when the communications began between Messrs. A. P. Sinnett and A. O. Hume and the Adepts, the word Master was applied to them, perhaps because both H.P.B. and Colonel Olcott used that word. But the Great Ones are not teachers, whose primary task is to give instruction in philosophy and to explain the problem of Liberation. They have made clear to us that their task is that of helping to diminish human misery, and that they concern themselves primarily with the millions of mankind *en masse*. Indeed one difficulty which arose between the European Theosophists and the Masters in 1880-4 was due to the fact that the former seemed constitutionally unable to realize that the Masters are not teachers to perform occult phenomena to convince a sceptical Western world, but the purest of philanthropists whose tireless work is to "lift a little of the heavy karma of the world ".

Do good works in his name

In all lands and at all times, the problem of the spiritual life is ever the same, because the fundamental laws of the soul's unfoldment do not change. But there are always variations in the themes which attempt to describe the life of the Spirit. There are in Indian religions two streams which run parallel to each other but rarely join. One stream is that of Charity. Indian religion inculcates pity and tenderness, and the need for a righteous man to be constantly aware of the problem of the distress of those who are poor, sick and suffering. The second stream is that which turns a soul's attention to its own Liberation.

One method in which this Liberation is sought is through a self-training in philosophic detachment, which does not keep in vision any Personal God who assists in the process. This is the theme of the Sankhya school of philosophers, of Buddhism, and of the "pure" Vedanta of Shankaracharya. A second method is through renunciation and devotion to a Personal God or Avatara, like Shri Krishna in Hinduism or Jesus Christ in Christianity. It is especially a characteristic of Hindu spiritual life that each man should seek his Liberation intently and as swiftly as possible, but not consecrate himself to relieve the needs of others, except in the general ways of charity and harmlessness. Hence the ideal of the Sannyasi in Hinduism, and of the Thera in Buddhism.

But it is a strong characteristic of the Christian spiritual life that the love of God should not be separated from charity to one's fellowmen. True, the monastic life has always been one ideal in Christianity ; yet Christianity has, more than any other religion, emphasized the close relation of social service to the worship of God. Even among Christian monks and nuns there are several Orders who devote themselves especially to the relief of suffering. This development has taken as its inspiration the words of the Christ, where He proclaims that He reveals His presence in those who are in need and suffering. " Forasmuch as ye have done it unto one of the least of these My brethren, ye have done it unto Me." From this has developed the ideal of a combination of devotion and action in the phrase, " In His Name ". We find therefore in Christianity a union of charity and worship ; the two can be made separate, but in the noblest Christian life they have ever been a unity.

It is to this conception of the practical life of the occultist, who seeks to serve the Master and at the same time is keenly aware of the needs of his fellowmen, that the Master K. H. refers in these striking words, " Do good works in his name ".

In India, especially, men think of a Master, not as a mere philosophical exponent of the spiritual life, but as one who is also the very incarnation of the Godhead as manifested in a physical body. The Godhead is therefore proclaimed as discoverable wherever the body of the Master can be found. So today in India, as in past ages, men wander from place to place "seeking the Guru". But when one realizes that each of the great Masters is in touch with every event in the world and in every place, through the use of the powers which are his as an Adept, then one knows that to "find the Guru" is not a matter of travelling from place to place, but of an inner change of heart and mind.

and for the love of mankind;

There is much charity practised, not for the love of *mankind*, but either for the love of God, or for "accumulating good karma." In certain Eastern religions the charitable man practises Dâna or giving, because he hopes thereby to acquire Punya or "merit", that is, good karma leading to Moksha or Nirvana. Among the Christian monastic and lay Orders who dedicate themselves to service, the beautiful offering of charity is made to please God and to serve Him, but not usually for the simple love of man. I recall vividly going through an institution for the aged in a country of Central America and being profoundly impressed by the patience of the nun in charge in dealing with refractory aged men and women. The forbearance shown was so great that I uttered a few words of admiration of the keen sense of human brotherhood shown by her. But her reply startled me : "We do it to please God". That it was true service and beautiful could not be gainsaid ; but it was not the "love of mankind", that tenderness to our fellowmen, just because they are men, which is implied in the Theosophical ideal of Brotherhood. It is this ideal of Brotherhood, "the love of mankind", which the Master K. H. exacts from those who aspire to become his chelas. He undoubtedly approves of charity done "to please God" ; such charity in no way detracts from chelaship. But the Master is a Bodhisattva, and it is only to those chelas who are filled with "the love of mankind" that he can pour out his love most, and make them his best agents.

as laid out in our rules

Every religion gives certain rules of conduct regarding what is the "Path of Righteousness". But as ages pass, the word

" Righteousness ", or Dharma as it is called in Sanskrit, is used to cover all kinds of actions and ceremonies which are proclaimed by priests and religious hierarchies as necessary for Righteousness or Dharma, but which have no relation to true Righteousness. Every religion is full of commandments supposed to have been given by a divine law-giver, but which historical investigations show are merely the result of the age-long accretions of priestly exploitation, or of the ignorant superstition of the peoples. There was a time in India when Sati, or the self-immolation of the widow on her husband's funeral pyre, was proclaimed by priests and law-makers as Dharma or the law of God. Up to only a few years ago in England, marriage with a deceased wife's sister was considered an outrage on morality and forbidden by law. The law is now changed, but the Church of England still will not allow such a marriage to be solemnized in its churches. Purdah or the veiling of women when in public, and in the home keeping them secluded away from the men, is proclaimed by Muslims as a commandment of the Prophet Muhammad and therefore of God. Polygamy is banned in some religions, but permitted in others. Sex taboos of various kinds claim a divine sanction, both among savage and civilized peoples. All civilization is full of customs which are permitted or not, according to the dictates of tradition and convention.

The Adept, however, is not concerned with the conventions of passing civilizations and creeds, but only with the fundamental realities which underlie right thought, feeling and action. The criterion of the Adept, as to the truth or untruth in every custom which is proclaimed as of God, is in the answer to the query : " Does it contain the germ of *cruelty* ? " Hence the use by the Master of the striking phrase " as laid out in *our* rules ", underlining the word " our ", drawing thereby special attention to the rules of the Adepts, and not to the rules of conventional custom or morality.

the periods of undisturbed progress

The Master has already alluded to the seven years of probation, which a chela can pass anywhere ; but that rule deals with the normal run of events. But there are certain periods of unusual stress, where the needs of the Great Work are especially urgent. In such abnormal circumstances, modifications of the normal rule take place. Such a crisis happened in 1884, when the Christian missionaries of Madras concocted a plot, with the help of two residents of the Theosophical Headquarters, to prove that H. P. B. had written, with her own hand, the letters from the Adepts, and that the existence of the Masters was a mere figment of her imagination which she foisted on her credulous disciples.

Now, H. P. B.'s work in starting the Theosophical Society at the bidding of the Masters was not a mere philosophical activity ; it was for the " Cause of Truth ", to use the Master's phrase. On the existence and the progress of the Society hung vast schemes of the Adepts for the regeneration of mankind. The attack by the missionaries on the Society, planning to destroy it, was an attack on mankind, however little they realized it. The missionaries thought they were doing " God service " ; but they were in reality doing exactly the contrary.

on its stand for life or death

It is necessary to dwell somewhat at length on this situation in 1884 of the Theosophical Society, to which the Master refers. I have just mentioned that there was an attack on the Society by the Christian missionaries of Madras. The genesis of the attack was as follows.

When in Cairo in 1871, H. P. B. became acquainted with a Frenchman, Monsieur Coulomb, and his English wife, who was Emma Cutting before her marriage. In 1878, H. P. B. and Colonel Olcott came to India and made Bombay the Headquarters of the Society. Somewhere about this time, the two Coulombs were in Galle, Ceylon, where they had opened a boarding house. This venture was about to collapse, when Madame Coulomb wrote to H. P. B. for a loan. H. P. B. replied that, if she cared to come to India with her husband, work would be found for them. So the two Coulombs came and were given what work was possible. The husband was good at carpentry, and a job was secured for him at a factory ; but he lost his job, and so work was found for him at the residence of the

Founders. Madame Coulomb was given the work of superintending the housekeeping. Later, Coulomb was put in charge of the small library of the Society, and his wife was given simple secretarial work. When the Founders left for Madras in 1882, the two Coulombs came with them and resided at the new Headquarters at Adyar.

In February, 1884, H. P. B. and Colonel Olcott left for Europe. The management of Headquarters was then put in the hands of a Board of Control. This Board soon found that Madame Coulomb was often trying to obtain loans from members who came to Adyar. Difficulties quickly arose between the Board of Control and Madame Coulomb, and finally the Board dismissed both husband and wife.

After the Founders left in February, no one resided in the upper part of the building, where was H. P. B.'s room. Adjoining it was a small room called the " Shrine Room ", where hung a collapsible wooden cabinet called the " Shrine ". It was in this " Shrine " that the Masters were wont to place their precipitated letters. For several weeks hardly anybody went upstairs except the Coulombs.

A plot was now hatched by them, which would enable them to revenge themselves on the Society and H. P. B. as already mentioned. Coulomb was an expert carpenter, and he contrived a wooden sliding panel at the back of the Shrine, and also made an opening in the wall behind it, with a second sliding panel. The wall at this spot was thin, as there was a " wall-cupboard " on the other side in H. P. B.'s room.

Here enters into the story one of its most disgraceful factors. This was the role played in the conspiracy by the Christian missionaries of Madras. Ever since the T. S. began its work in India, the revival of Indian religion and culture had of course begun to put obstacles in the way of missionary effort. Each year that passed made missionary activities harder, because the Founders of the T. S. and their band of workers inspired the Hindus to revive their ancient culture, and the Buddhists of Ceylon to revive Buddhism. Sanskrit schools had been established in India, and vernacular schools in Ceylon. Translations of Hindu and Buddhist scriptures had been begun, and so a counter-propaganda to missionary proselytization was started.

When therefore the two Coulombs came to the missionaries, with their story of a sliding panel in the Shrine, the missionaries saw an excellent opportunity to annihilate the Theosophical Society and its work. They took up the Coulombs, financed them, and an attack was launched on the Society in the missionary magazine. So-called evidence was offered to prove that the Masters were an invention of H. P. B., and that the letters phenomenally produced in the Shrine were written by H. P. B., and placed there by the Coulombs with her connivance. At the same time letters, which were forged by the Coulombs, purporting to be in H. P. B.'s handwriting, were produced to show that the idea of the Masters was mere trickery on the part of H. P. B.

The story of the Coulombs was that, at H. P. B.'s suggestion, Coulomb had made the sliding panel in the Shrine, and the opening to it from the other side. So obviously the letters were not placed mysteriously in the Shrine by the Masters, but were written by H. P. B. with her own hand, and placed in the Shrine through the secret aperture in her room.

Now, dozens of people had for several months before H. P. B.'s departure not only seen the Shrine, but had also examined it carefully; they knew that there was no sliding panel at the back of the Shrine, nor did the wall where it hung have any communication with the room on the other side. To those therefore who had examined the Shrine, it was clear that, after H. P. B.'s departure, when there was no one in the upper floor of the house, Coulomb had contrived the panels.

This was the situation of the Society, when it was, in the Master's words, " on its stand for life or death before the tribunal of public opinion—that most flippantly cruel, prejudiced and unjust of all tribunals ".

It may well be asked, if the Masters are in such close touch with the world's affairs, how it was that they were unable to foresee this missionary attack upon the Society. *They did foresee it*, as too the shock to the Society which it entailed. In a letter, precipitated in a railway compartment in motion, which Colonel Olcott received in England on April 5, 1884, the following appears.

" Do not be surprised at anything you may hear from Adyar, nor discouraged. It is possible—we try to prevent it within the limits of karma—that you may have great domestic annoyances to pass through. You have harboured a traitor and an enemy under your roof for years, and the missionary party are more than ready to avail of any help she may be induced to give. A regular conspiracy is on foot. She is maddened by the appearance of Mr. Lane Fox and the powers you have given to the Board of Control.

" We have been doing some phenomena at Adyar since H. P. B. left, to protect Upasika from the conspirators." [1]

If the Masters foresaw the attack, why did they not prevent it ? The answer is already given by the Master : " within the limits of karma ". Mistakes made by even their most trusted agents must come to their due results. With delicate hints and subtle warnings, but of such a nature as not to force the will of their agent, the Masters do indicate possible danger. But if the hint is not taken and an error in technique is made, they will not interfere to prevent the consequences.

There is a second reason why the Masters—once that the effect is set in motion by a cause—only watch, and do not interfere. It is to " divide the sheep from the goats ", to use the Christian simile. The Masters have utilized the disturbances among the Society's members to see who are those who stand for principles and who for persons. When the Society is attacked from without, or the clashes of their personal karmas make bitter divisions among the members, the Masters note that those for whom Theosophy—the " Cause of Truth "—is closely associated *with a personality*, leave the Society at a crisis, because their faith in the integrity of that person is shaken, owing to what appear to be proofs of his unworthiness ; but they note also that there are others, for whom the Great Philosophy, and especially the work for Universal Brotherhood, are based on principles, and not on persons. These latter stand by the Society in every emergency, and carry on the crippled work. It is to select these for greater fields of service that the Adepts, however much they regret the confusion in the public mind and the waste of energy of the members in unfraternal life, allow without interfering the interplay of the karmic forces of the members.

[1] *Letters from the Masters of the Wisdom*, First Series, Letter XVIII.

For the future of the Society depends upon those who put first loyalty to the Theosophical Ideals, and then only afterwards devotion to persons whom they revere as leaders and teachers.

But often principles and personalities are so interwoven in a man's mind that it requires " a well developed Intuition " to separate the one from the other. This is one of the problems which the occultist has to solve.

Another factor in this problem is that the Masters are *not* anxious that all in the world should be convinced of their existence. Their work and that of their agents, the Master K. H. has said, is

> " not for those who are unwilling to part with their prejudices and preconceptions for the attainment of truth from whatever source it may come. It is not our desire to convince the latter, for no fact or explanation can make a blind man see. Moreover our existence would become extremely intolerable, if not impossible, were all persons indiscriminately *convinced*." [1]

flippantly cruel

Those who read the letters of the Master K. H., who have a fine appreciation of the meaning of English words, will note again and again the remarkable acquaintance which the Master has of the nuances of English phrasing. No phrase so precise and apt as " flippantly cruel " could describe the gusts of public anger which are directed upon a man or woman in public life, when the feelings of the " public " are fanned to fury by an appeal to their prejudices. With a sense of irresponsibility which characterizes savages, the public try to tear in pieces such a victim of their anger. But there is a flippancy in it all, for when a new victim is offered to them, or some other new excitement to their emotions, the old deeds, and with them the havoc created, are forgotten.

There is a phrase that a man can be " hounded to his death ". A man so persecuted does indeed sometimes break down utterly and make away with himself, or at least renounce his work, unable to " carry on " against the mad persecution of the public. But there are valiant souls who refuse to be hounded to their death.

---

[1] *Letters from the Masters of the Wisdom*, First Series, Letter XXII.

Such was H. P. B. So too was Annie Besant. Not less in firmness and in refusal to be driven out of his work for the Master was C. W. Leadbeater. In 1906-7 many so-called " Theosophists " tried to drive him out of the Theosophical field of service ; later, he has been hooted at by ragamuffins in the streets of Sydney, stirred thereto by the gutter-press of the city, and yet " not turned a hair ", as is the phrase, but gone serenely on his way to his work, without the slightest feeling of resentment, as if the hooters were no more than the flies which pester us in these lands and which we brush away with our hands.

the collective karma of <u>the caste you belong to</u>

As is clear from what has gone before, it was the representatives of Christianity who were making an attempt to destroy utterly the Theosophical Society ; but these missionaries were not of the Church of England, to which Mr. Leadbeater belonged.

The Master for the first time reveals a fact that no one had thought of before—that there is not only individual karma, but also a collective karma of a group, like a caste or a nation. While Mr. Leadbeater took no part in the missionary plot to destroy the Society, and on the contrary was a staunch supporter of it, nevertheless, since he too was a minister of Christ, he also was involved in the karma of the Madras Christian missionaries. Now, Mr. Leadbeater as a Church of England priest, who denied that Wesleyans, Baptists, Congregationalists and similar " Nonconformists " who were attacking the Society were true " priests " at all, because they did not have the " Apostolic succession " as he did, could not have realized, before receiving the Master's letter, that he too had his share in the attack on the Society.

Are you willing to atone for <u>their</u> sins?

Until Mr. Leadbeater had in some manner purified himself from the " sin " of his caste, so that the forces of the Master could act through him without obstruction, it was of little use to look forward to become a chela soon. How could he purify himself ?

By going to Madras, the very camp of the missionary plotters, and by showing publicly that an ordained priest of Christ was heart and soul with the Society. Such an action would atone for the sins of his fellow-Christians, so far as his lot in their karma was concerned.

" The ties of gratitude "

Mr. Leadbeater had mentioned, in the letter sent through " Ernest ", that much as he would like to give himself immediately to the Society, " ties of gratitude " held him back from such a course of action. As has been explained already, he was a curate in the parish of his uncle, the Rev. W. W. Capes. He owed much to his uncle, who had helped him financially and otherwise to enter the Christian ministry, and found a post for him as curate from the day of his admission as a deacon. For several years afterwards, he and his mother lived at Bramshott, and naturally there were close relations between the Leadbeaters and the Rectory. To go out to India would distinctly mean to sever the ties of gratitude which bound him to his benefactor. And Mr. Leadbeater felt, in March 1884 when he wrote to the Master, that he could not do it.

if the step be explained plausibly,

The Master suggested " an absence of a few months." Mr. Leadbeater had one very " plausible " reason for such a brief visit to India, had he cared to take it. There was at this time in India a great schoolboy chum of his, to whom he had a deep attachment ; this friend was acting as the captain of a coast to coast steamer of the British India Steam Navigation Company, and a standing invitation to come and visit him had been with Mr. Leadbeater for some years.

the years of probation

The word " probation "—which means to *prove* oneself—was used in these early days in a sense somewhat different from that attached to it later. Since about 1889, probation came to mean the formal admission of the aspirant as a " chela ", that is, as one of the Master's selected band. It is at this moment of admission that the Master makes the " living image " of the chela, and examines it periodically to note how the chela's character is changing. But there is a preliminary stage, during which the aspirant is kept under observation, but no responsibility is undertaken by the Master towards him, as in the case of a chela.

It is to this preliminary stage, usually of a period of seven years, that the Master refers, when he said that " the seven years of probation " can be passed " anywhere ". We shall see later that Mr. Leadbeater reduced the period to less than twelve *hours*, and became a chela.

to make sacrifices for theosophy

The Master has alluded to the fact that progress on the Occult Path " can only be the result of one's personal merit and exertions in that direction." The aspirant must " knock " at the door of the Master by deeds of self-sacrifice ; he must have created such an accumulation of karma on the good side that he proves that he has stepped out of the ranks of the many, and is offering to join the small band of those who are pledged " to lift a little the heavy karma of the world." Just as in the case of a boat going upstream through a lock, and is already inside the lock, the lock has to be filled before its gates leading to the higher level of water can be opened, so similarly the aspirant must have created a sufficient force of karma before the " gates " which lead to the entrance to the Path will open. It is by sacrifices of various kinds, involving discomfort, suffering, renunciation, etc., in a noble cause, that the idealist increases his " stock of good karma."

In these days, the idea of " sacrifice " sounds strange in connection with joining the Theosophical Society, or working for its ideals. The Theosophical ideas are so widespread, and in India and in English-speaking lands, like Britain and the United States to-day, not considered so outrageous, that little sacrifice is involved if a seeker for the higher life determines to associate himself with Theosophists. But it was not so in the early days of the Society. About the eighties of the last century, in many countries (except India) for a man to be a Theosophist was to be considered a little mad, and in some Christian lands where fanaticism was still alive, to court persecution. All this has changed in Britain, in most countries of Europe, and in the United States.

But it is not so yet in " Latin America ", that is, the twenty republics of South and Central America, Mexico, Cuba, the Dominican Republic and Puerto Rico. In these countries, where Protestant influence is scarcely to be felt in social or public life, the power of the Church of Rome is still a ruthless autocracy over its adherents. I know from personal experience during two long tours working in those lands for Theosophy, how the priests have invariably tried, not only subtly but sometimes also openly, to suppress Theosophical propaganda, especially by threatening the women members of the Church with religious penalties if they attended my lectures. Theosophy has been officially banned by name by the Pope as a dire heresy, and in one month in each year, a prayer is offered to God through the Virgin Mary to save the world from Theosophy.

In these countries, it does require an act of sacrifice on the part of a seeker for truth to identify himself openly with Theosophy and the Theosophical Society. However, if a man or woman shows a bold front to the priests, they will give the Theosophist up as a " bad job ", warning all however that the wicked son or daughter of the Church will be condemned to eternal perdition. Yet, so subtle is the influence of the Roman Catholic priests, that many a man and woman in Latin America has to undergo a veiled persecution which affects both his or her material prosperity and family relations. What Christ said in Palestine is still true, concerning the opposition which the earnest seeker will meet : " A man's foes shall be they of his own household."

If the earnest seeker is loyal to the dictates of his higher self, and bravely meets persecution, then he will prove, as many have proved who have braved public opinion and the hostility of family and friends, what the Master K. H. has said.

> " He who damns himself in his own estimation and agreeably
> to the recognised and current code of honour to save a
> worthy cause may some day find out that he has reached
> thereby his loftiest aspirations.

3

" Selfishness and the want of self-sacrifice are the greatest
impediments on the path of adeptship."[1]

What were the sacrifices which Mr. Leadbeater made for Theosophy we shall see later.

theosophy

One striking fact, in the voluminous teachings given by the
Adepts in the early days of the Society, is how rarely the word
Theosophy appears, as the designation of the teachings which they
offered.   In my two compilations, *The Letters from the Masters of the
Wisdom* (First and Second Series), the word appears only four times,
and twice in this letter to Mr. Leadbeater.   In the large volume of the
letters of the Masters M. and K. H. to Mr. Sinnett, compiled by
Mr. A. T. Barker in *The Mahatma Letters to A. P. Sinnett*, the word
appears only seven times.   The word is of course now used by all,
including the public, as a label to describe a set of ideas held by a
body of people who profess (so thinks the public) a new faith.   But
it is clear, as we read the letters of the Adepts, that it is not the name
that matters, but truths and principles which are eternal and unchang-
ing, whatever label is given to them in successive civilizations.

Twice in this letter, and three times in other letters the Master
writes " theosophy ", with a small " t ".   We have to note that
capital letters do not exist in the Devanagari script used for Sanskrit,
nor in any scripts derived from it in any vernacular language
of India.   The word of course is Greek, a language which has no
capitals, or rather, in which all the letters were capitals, in the early
form of the script.

The word first appears in Proclus, the Neo-Platonic teacher of
Alexandria (born 410 A. D.), when he speaks of " the theosophy of
foreign peoples ", to describe their beliefs as to the existence of
the gods.[2]

Whenever the Masters speak of the " Theosophical Society ",
the " T. S.", the " Society ", and the " Founders " (meaning only
H. P. B. and Colonel Olcott), capitals are always used.

[1] *Letters from the Masters of the Wisdom*, First Series, Letter X.

[2] The Greek words used by Proclus are given in a footnote on pp. 19-20 by T. Whittaker
in his work, *The Neo-Platonists*.

A very noteworthy fact is that, though the Theosophical Society was originated by the Masters, and is their messenger to the world, and they have guided it in its chequered career, there is *no mention of the word Theosophy* in the Constitution of the Society which regulates the work of its constituent parts, the National Societies or " Sections." There is *no official definition* of what is Theosophy. Therefore every member of the Society can claim the right, under the Constitution, to declare what Theosophy is, or what it is not. For the work of the Society is not primarily to proclaim a cut-and-dried philosophy, but to establish a Universal Brotherhood.

It is by <u>doing</u> noble actions

The emphasis which the Master makes upon the word " *doing* ", by underlining it, is a sharp reminder that the time for dreaming, hoping and planning is over. In a letter to Miss F. Arundale he describes how beautiful and unselfish dreams have a higher origin than the mind of the lower self.

> " Good resolutions are mind-painted pictures of good
> *deeds* : fancies, day-dreams, whisperings of the *Buddhi* to
> the manas." [1]

It may well have been that, when emphasizing action, the Master was reminded of Carlyle's words, " The end of Man is an Action, and not a Thought ", for immediately afterwards we have a quotation from Carlyle.

Like the " true man " of Carlyle

One interesting fact about the Master K. H. is that he has evidently read widely in Western literature, for in many of his letters we find quotations or references to them. In one letter he quotes from the *Light of Asia*, in another from Tennyson, and in a letter by the Master M. asks the latter to quote to Mr. Sinnett the first verse of the well-known poem of Christina Rossetti, " Does the road wind uphill all the way ? " An unusual quotation is from a Danish poet.[2]

---

[1] *Letters from the Masters of the Wisdom*, Letter XX.
[2] *Letters from the Masters of the Wisdom*, Second Series, Letter 77,

One reference which has been difficult to locate was to a statement of the Greek philosopher Anaxagoras ; it was traced finally by a friend of mine, a professor of Greek.

The quotation from Carlyle is as follows :

> " to be seduced by ease, difficulty, abnega-
> tion, martyrdom, death are the <u>allurements</u>
> that act "

It is evident that the Master has read Carlyle's *Heroes and Hero Worship*, for it is in Carlyle's lecture on " The Hero as Prophet " that the following sentences appear.

> " It is a calumny on men to say that they are roused to heroic action by ease, hope of pleasure, recompense, sugar-plums of any kind, in this world or the next ! In the meanest mortal there lies something nobler. The poor swearing soldier, hired to be shot, has his ' honour of a soldier,' different from drill-regulations and the shilling a day. It is not to taste sweet things, but to do noble and true things, and vindicate himself under God's Heaven as a god-made Man, that the poorest son of Adam dimly longs. Show him the way of doing that, the dullest daydrudge kindles into a hero. They wrong man greatly who say he is to be seduced by ease. Difficulty, abnegation, martyrdom, death are the *allurements* that act on the heart of man. Kindle the inner genial life of him, you have a flame that burns up lower considerations."

Especially noteworthy is the underlining by the Master of the word *allurements*. One could easily suppose that he underlined the word so as to draw Mr. Leadbeater's attention to those sacrifices, which the ordinary man would consider grievous, but which the " true man " will always consider privileges. But the italicizing of the word has a more interesting reason than that, which is, that Carlyle himself italicizes the word. It is not unusual for a student and writer when he discovers a striking phrase to remember its words ; but it is hardly ever that he will remember what words in the phrase are underlined, that is, are in italics. It is therefore reasonable to suppose that, as the Master quoted Carlyle, he had *Heroes and Hero Worship* before him, and quoted not from memory but direct from tho book itself.

the " true man "

As the Master quotes Carlyle, he makes a very significant change. Carlyle writes, " a god-made Man "; the Master writes the " the true man ". The change is not accidental, but of set purpose.

In all the communications from the Masters, in the period 1880-8, they object to the use of the word " God ", as a designation to describe the Ultimate Reality, the Root Cause, the Substratum, which is the basis of the universe and the Primary Cause of every-thing. Because, as can be seen everywhere, the word God at once connotes a *Personal* God, that is, a Creator, a Manipulator of the universe, who is imaged in a human form (though he may have many heads and arms as in Hindu images). Once the Ultimate Reality is so personalized, the next invariable result is to offer prayers to him, asking him for benefits or for exemption from the operation of his own laws.

It is obvious that the mind of man, infinitesimal compared to the vastness of the universe, cannot make anything but a distorted image of a personalized God. One evil result—not necessarily in-evitable, but certainly very common—is that man loses sight of that fact which it is absolutely essential for him to know—that he lives in a universe of immutable and utterly dependable laws. When this supreme fact is placed in the background of man's consciousness, and *not* in its foreground, there is a natural attempt to " get round " Karma, the Law of Cause and Effect, by invoking the aid of a capricious agent who is outside that law.

It is this personalized conception of Ultimate Reality which brings swiftly in its train many an evil as, for instance, the rivalries of the religions which name the Reality under different names, proclaim an exclusive salvation to those who worship it under only one especial name, and fight fiercely as to which is the one and only true God.

Should, however, the Reality be so concretized and personal-ized, a natural spring in the human heart is to worship Him. But with such a worship come priesthoods and ceremonies, which may assist the soul in worship, or on the other hand may cramp and limit that soul in its worship, as so often happens when priests and priestcrafts take command over the human heart.

On this point the great Adept known as the Mahachohan declared once :

"Once unfettered and delivered from their deadweight of dogmatic interpretations, personal names, anthropomorphic conceptions and salaried priests, the fundamental doctrines of all religions will be proved identical in their esoteric meaning. Osiris, Krishna, Buddha, Christ, will be shown as different names for one and the same royal highway to final bliss—NIRVANA. Mystical Christianity, that is to say, that Christianity which teaches self-redemption through our own Seventh principle—this liberated Para-Atma (Augoeides) called by some Christ, by others Buddha, and equivalent to regeneration or rebirth in Spirit—will be found just the same truth as the Nirvana of Buddhism."[1]

The great Adept said also :

" The world in general, and Christendom especially, left for 2,000 years to the régime of a personal God, as well as its political and social systems based on that idea, has now proved a failure ".[1]

No less striking is the Adept's assertion that the increasing struggle for existence—how greatly it has increased since he wrote in 1881 we can all note—is due to the stress which the religions, which proclaim a Personal God, have made up on the dread of death.

" As we find the world now, whether Christian, Mussulman, or Pagan, justice is disregarded and honour and mercy both flung to the winds. In a word, how—seeing that the main objects of the T. S. are misinterpreted by those who are most willing to serve us personally—are we to deal with the rest of mankind, with that curse known as the ' struggle for life ', which is the real and most prolific parent of most woes and sorrows and all crimes ? Why has that struggle become the almost universal scheme of the universe ? We answer, because no religion, with the exception of Buddhism, has hitherto taught a practical

[1] *Letters from the Masters of the Wisdom*, First Series, Letter I.

contempt for the earthly life, while each of them, always with that one solitary exception, has through its hells and damnations inculcated the greatest dread of death. Therefore do we find that struggle for life raging most fiercely in Christian countries, most prevalent in Europe and America. It weakens in the Pagan lands, and is nearly unknown among Buddhist populations. . . . Teach the people to see that life on this earth, even the happiest, is but a burden and delusion, that it is but our own Karma, the cause producing the effect, that is our own judge, our saviour in future lives, and the great struggle for life will soon lose its intensity".[1]

It must not be supposed that the Adepts proclaim that there is no " God " ; such a declaration would lead to the rankest Materialism, which is the very negation of their philosophy. One Adept, the Master " Serapis ", in his communications to Colonel Olcott in 1875, four times invokes " God's blessing " on him, at the conclusion of his letters.

The two greatest philosophers of Hinduism, Shankaracharya and Ramanujacharya, the heads of two different philosophical schools expounding *the same Vedanta teaching*, are divided on this point, whether the Ultimate Reality is to be conceived only as an absolute Impersonal Principle, or as one capable at the same time of revealing itself as a Personal God, *without losing its attributes as the Absolute*. The " non-dual ", " pure " Vedanta represented by Shankaracharya asserts the illimitable, unsurpassable Divinity of that Principle, the very essence of Being, Bliss and Intelligence ; but THAT is not different in nature from the human Soul, or to put it more accurately, the Soul and THAT are *always* one and inseparable, however separate the Soul appears to be when it functions as an embodied being. But the philosophy of Ramanujacharya insists that while the Soul and THAT are ever one, nevertheless there is an aspect of the Absolute which is the Personal God, which the Soul can worship for ever and ever *after* Liberation, while still united to THAT. This philosophy asserts the complete identity of Soul with God, yet " with a difference."

[1] *Letters from the Masters of the Wisdom*, First Series, Letter I.

The answer which Buddhism makes to this intricate and lofty problem has been given accurately by Edwin Arnold in his *Light of Asia*, in the opening verse with which he introduces the First Sermon preached by Buddha after Enlightenment.

> OM, AMITAYA ![1] measure not with words
> Th' Immeasurable ; nor sink the string of thought
> Into the Fathomless.   Who asks doth err,
> Who answers, errs.   Say naught !

Nevertheless, the mistrust of the Adepts to use the word God—as now used in ordinary speech—must not be construed as denying the existence of the GODS, Beings so supreme in their splendour, power and love as to serve " for us men and for our salvation " the place of God, whom we can worship in uttermost devotion, and be brought nearer to our Liberation by that worship.   But these— Dhyan Chohans, Planetary Logoi, Solar Logoi—are still *within* the Law of the Ultimate Reality.   There is the Great Being who is the Mainspring and Mainstay of all within the Solar System, whom we call the Solar Logos ; in Him we " live and move and have our being."   Yet beyond Him are greater Logoi still.   As to the nature of the Ultimate Reality in which the Logoi themselves " live and move and have their being ", who has the right to proclaim what IT is *not* ?

If I were to demand

These words of the Master have a very great significance. Since we are beginners, we want constantly to be guided by those whom we regard as " elders " ; our devotion to them is great and therefore we are utterly ready to carry out their orders.   In Occultism, however, the problem is not that of blind obedience to the code of another, but of " grasping one's own destiny ", as the Master says at the conclusion of this letter.

It is true that, in our desire never to err from the Path, and especially not to make complications for the work of the Master, we feel the need of the advice of an elder ; yet it is the fact that we must ourselves find the true road by our own discrimination and intuition. We may, and do, often err ; nevertheless, if our heart is pure and our

---

[1] The Sanskrit word Amitaya means " what cannot be measured ".

motive has been for unselfish service, any error which we make will create comparatively speaking only a slight karma of confusion and evil. This can be compensated for by us by deeds of helpfulness. In the meantime, even if we have blundered somewhat, we shall have grown in power of decision and discrimination by relying upon ourselves.

Mr. Leadbeater asked what he was to *do*, in order to be received as a chela. The Master does not direct him, for Mr. Leadbeater must act on his own initiative for the operation of Karma to be precise and unalloyed. We shall see, in the second letter from the Master, when Mr. Leadbeater had decided upon his course of action, and the Master accepts him as a chela, that the Master does then specify what are the actions which he requires of his new chela. But at the early stage of receiving the first letter, when the Master explains in outline the problems of probation and of the need to help to save the Society, Mr. Leadbeater alone must " cast the lot yourself into the lap of Justice, never fearing but that its response will be absolutely true."

shall end in adeptship or failure.

The Master stated at the end of 1882 that of those would-be-chelas who had been put on probation and tested that year, half of them had failed. In a letter to Colonel Olcott the Master writes :

" Why must I even now (to put your thoughts in the right channel) remind you of the three cases of *insanity* within seven months among ' lay chelas ', not to mention one's turning a thief ? " [1]

Referring to one of these, who desired to be accepted as a chela by the Master M., the Master K. H. writes :

" The option of receiving him or not as a regular chela— remains with the Chohan. M. has simply to have him tested, tempted and examined by all and every means, so as to have his real nature drawn out. This is a rule with us as inexorable as it is disgusting in your Western sight, and I could not prevent it even if I would. It is not enough

[1] *The Mahatma Letters to A. P. Sinnett*, Letter LXVII.

to know thoroughly what the chela is capable of doing or not doing at the time and the circumstances during the period of probation. We have to know of what he *may* become capable under different and every kind of opportunities ".[1]

Explaining that this process of testing is applied to all, and referring to yet another failure in another letter, that of an Englishman who was converted to Muhammadanism, Moorad Ali Beg, the Master writes :

" What has happened to Fern has befallen every one else who has preceded, and will befall with various results every one who succeeds him. We were all so tested ; and while a Moorad Ali—*failed*—I, succeeded." [2]

Little wonder, then, that the Master wrote :

" Sigh not for Chelaship ; pursue not that, the dangers and hardships of which are unknown to you. Verily many are the chelas offering themselves to us, and as many have failed this year as were accepted on probation. Chelaship unveils the inner man and draws forth the dormant virtue as well as the dormant vice. Latent vice begets active sins and is often followed by insanity. Throw a glance round, make an enquiry at Bareilly and Cawnpore, and judge for yourself. Be pure, virtuous, and lead a holy life and you will be protected. But remember, he who is not as pure as a young child better leave chelaship alone." [3]

During the period that I have been closely connected with the work of the Masters, there have been among the pupils of the Masters three suicides and one attempted suicide. As to those whose failures have taken other forms, " their number is legion ". It is still true as of old, " Many be called, but few chosen."

Chelas, from a mistaken idea of our system,

The idea prevalent in India of the relation between the Guru (teacher) and his Shishya (pupil) implies that the pupil is on

---

[1] *The Mahatma Letters to A. P. Sinnett,* Letter XXX.
[2] *The Mahatma Letters to A. P. Sinnett,* Letter LIV.
[3] *Letters from the Masters of the Wisdom,* First Series, Letter IX.

attendance on his teacher, ready to serve him in every way. With this conception goes the corollary that the pupil must do nothing without his teacher's instructions. All this is reasonable if one starts with the notion that the pupil's task is to be a humble server of the Master.

But in Occultism the idea is somewhat different. A Master of the Wisdom does not require a band of disciples round him to serve him in his personal needs, nor to be merely pupils to be taught by him religion and philosophy in return. An Adept is fundamentally, by his status, an agent in the Plan of the Logos; for him it is the fact that " I and my Father are one." He is therefore an organizer of the divine energies, a distributing station of the powers which the Plan of the Logos holds for mankind.

A Master therefore does not seek mere disciples, but rather *apprentices* who can be swiftly trained to be efficient and reliable assistants. These must necessarily become attuned to the spirit of every thought and deed of their " chief." They must therefore undergo a definite training and an exacting discipline. But, just as the Master himself is an agent of the Divine Plan, so must each disciple of his become quickly an agent of the Master's plans in that department of the Great Work which is entrusted to the Master's care.

A pupil needs on the one hand to be docile, that is, be what the Latin world describes, *teachable* ; but also on the other hand he must show initiative. For the pupil himself is also some day to become a Master. He must therefore possess a capacity to direct and command.

Certainly a Master gives directions to a pupil, and sometimes, as we shall see in the second letter received by Mr. Leadbeater, very precise directions. In the main, however, a Master outlines the work to be done by the pupil, and what are the final results which he expects from that work. But he leaves the pupil alone to make his own experiments regarding how he will achieve the objective set before him.

This throws upon the pupil a responsibility which he thinks he cannot bear ; he would far rather that the Master gave orders affecting *all* that he, the pupil, is to do. This of course would make of the pupil a mere mechanical tool of the Master, which is the last thing which any Master desires. Constantly today in India, would-be workers for the Theosophical Society come to some of us and say, " I have come to serve. Will you tell me what to do ? " When in reply we ask the question, " What can you do ? ", the unsatisfactory reply is given, " Anything ", which is an indication to an experienced employer that the applicant for work is inefficient in most things, though full of willingness to serve.

In Occultism, the pupil, while always " docile "—that is, teach-able and eager to obey every command of his Master—and alert to every suggestion made to him, has ever to be ready to devise and carry through his own plans as he tries to serve his Master. Hence the Master's words, " Chelas from a mistaken idea of our system, too often watch and wait for orders, wasting precious time which should be taken up with personal effort."

our Lord's the Tathâgata's memory

This phrase has long puzzled me, and I do not know that I have yet correctly the interpretation of the Master's thought. If the *blessing* of the Tathâgata—the Buddhist title for the Lord Gautama Buddha—had been invoked, the explanation would be simple, though it would seem strange to invoke that particular blessing upon a Christian clergyman. But what is the " memory " of the Lord which is in-voked ? The phrase suggests that somewhere in the past Mr. Lead-beater had met the Lord Buddha. In this life he had read *The Light of Asia*, and so knew the term Tathâgata, as also the life of the Lord narrated in the poem. But it could not be to the memory of a character in a poem that the Master was appealing.

No doubt he had met the Lord, as thousands of us, in many a previous incarnation of His as the Bodhisattva. Somewhere in our Ego-nature such a beautiful memory must lie dormant, and can be awakened. If such were the case, then, on such an occasion as this, when the decision made by Mr. Leadbeater would influence him for many lives, that memory could, if awakened, be a great source of illumination to the Ego.

Up to the year 1909, Mr. Leadbeater knew the details of his incarnation as a Greek in Athens ; but he was not in incarnation in

India at the time that the Lord Buddha was giving His great teaching, though some of Mr. Leadbeater's fellow-workers like Dr. Annie Besant and myself were there. But in the investigations into the past lives of " Alcyone ", a very significant occasion was found when Mr. Leadbeater did meet the Lord. A full description of this incident is given in *The Lives of Alcyone*, Life V.[1] The Tathâgata, in a life which He lived about 40,000 B.C., travelled from the City of the White Island in Central Asia to Egypt. In Egypt He taught the Atlantean priesthood there the Mystery Teaching of the Hidden Light and the Hidden Work. Egyptian legends later spoke of Him as Thoth or Téhuti, called in Greek tradition Hermes Trismegistus—Hermes the Thrice Greatest.

On His return from Egypt towards His home in Central Asia, He stayed for a while in Arabia, where His Brother, the Manu of the Fifth Root Race, had come with His hosts, and was arranging the colonization of His second or Arabian sub-race. There were born at the time, and as members of the same family, five Egos whose destiny is to become great teachers in the future, following the " Ray of the Buddhas ".

After a period during which the Lord gave His teachings to selected descendants of the Manu, He called before Him at a valedictory meeting these five (one of whom was the Ego called C. W. Leadbeater in this incarnation of his), and gave them the following " charge " regarding their future work.

> " Hail ! my Brother through the ages ; hail ! my brothers yet to be ; you shall spread God's Love and Wisdom o'er the world from sea to sea. Many and great shall be your difficulties and trials, yet greater still shall be your reward ; for many thousands of years you must toil in preparation for the task that few can undertake, but when it is achieved you shall shine as the stars in heaven, for yours is the blessing of those who turn many to righteousness. There is a spiritual dynasty whose throne is never vacant, whose splendour never fails ; its members form a golden chain whose links can never be torn asunder, for they draw back the world to God from whom it came. To that you all belong ;

[1] *The Lives of Alcyone*, pp. 64-66.

its labour and its lustre you must share. Happy are you among men, my Brothers of the Glorious Mystery, for through you the Light shall shine. More and more shall the Hidden Light become manifest ; more and more shall the Hidden Work be done openly and be understood by men ; and yours shall be the hands that raise the veil, yours the voices that shall proclaim the glad tidings to the world. Bearers of freedom and light and joy shall you be, and your names shall be holy in the ears of generations yet unborn. Farewell ; in this body you will see me no more, but forget not that in spirit we are always together."

With this invocation to the Highest in C. W. Leadbeater to *remember*, and to be guided by that memory " to decide for the best ", the letter ends with the initials " K. H." of the name Koot Hoomi, which is not the Master's personal name, but the title of his office as a high dignitary of the Koothoompa [1] sect of Tibetan Buddhism.

---

[1] But pronounced Kethoomba, the Master informs Mohini Chatterjee in Letter 59, *The Letters from the Masters of the Wisdom*, Second Series.

THE SECOND LETTER OF THE MASTER K. H.

As has already been mentioned, on the evening of October 30th the Master D. K. sent Mr. Leadbeater a message through H. P. B. that the Master K. H. had dispatched an answer to his (Mr. Leadbeater's) letter of March 3rd. Nothing was said as to the nature of the reply. Leaving London on the morning of October 31st, Mr. Leadbeater reached his home at Bramshott about one o'clock. There awaited him a letter, addressed in ink in the usual manner, " The Rev. C. W. Leadbeater, Liphook, Hants."[1] The letter inside was in blue pencil handwriting, and we have seen what it said.

Mr. Leadbeater decided quickly. But H. P. B. was leaving London next morning on her way to India, and many things had to be settled. He was the manager of the local Church school, where one of his young friends, Frank W. Matley, was a pupil teacher. A younger brother, James W. Matley, was in one of the classes. Mr. Leadbeater went to the school to give various instructions, as he had decided to return to London by the 3.56 train that same afternoon. On returning home he wrote then his second letter to the Master K. H., in reply to the Master's communication, and took it with him to London. Here we have the story of the next events in this striking drama from Mr. Leadbeater himself.

" I wished to say in answer to this that my circumstances were such that it would be impossible for me to come to Adyar for three months, and then return to the work in which I was then engaged ; but that I was perfectly ready to throw up that work altogether, and to devote my life absolutely to His service. Ernest having so conspicuously failed me,

[1] A reproduction of the envelope is given later.

I knew of no way to send this message to the Master but to take it to Madame Blavatsky, and as she was to leave England on the following day for India, I hastened up to London to see her.

" It was with difficulty that I induced her to read the letter [1], as she said very decidedly that such communications were intended only for the recipient. I was obliged to insist, however, and at last she read it and asked me what I wished to say in reply. I answered to the above effect, and asked her how this information could be conveyed to the Master. She replied that He knew it already, referring of course to the exceedingly close relation in which she stood with Him, so that whatever was within her consciousness was also within His when He wished it.

" She then told me to wait by her, and not to leave her on any account. She adhered absolutely to this condition, even making me accompany her into her bedroom when she went to put on her hat and, when a cab was required, declining me to allow me to leave the room and go to the door to whistle for it. I could not at all understand the purpose of this at the time, but afterwards I realized that she wished me to be able to say that she had never been out of my sight for a moment, between the time when she read my letter from the Master and my receipt of the reply to it. I remember as vividly as if it were yesterday how I rode with her in that hansom cab, and the bashful embarrassment that I felt, caused partly by the honour of doing so, and partly by my fear that I must be inconveniencing her horribly, for I was crushed sideways into a tiny corner of the seat, while her huge bulk weighed down her side of the vehicle, so that the springs were grinding all through the journey. Mr. and Mrs. Cooper-Oakley were to accompany her on the voyage to India, and it was to their house that I went with her very late that night—in fact, I believe it was after midnight, so I really ought to say very early the next morning.

[1] The *first* letter of the Master K. H., received that day.

My first phenomenon

" Even at that hour a number of devoted friends were gathered in Mrs. Oakley's drawing-room to say farewell to Madame Blavatsky, who seated herself in an easy-chair by the fireside. She was talking brilliantly to those who were present, and rolling one of her eternal cigarettes, when suddenly her right hand was jerked out towards the fire in a very peculiar fashion, and lay palm upwards. She looked down at it in surprise, as I did myself, for I was standing close to her, leaning with an elbow on the mantlepiece : and several of us saw quite clearly a sort of whitish mist form in the palm of her hand and then condense into a piece of folded paper, which she at once handed to me, saying : " There is your answer." Every one in the room crowded round, of course, but she sent me away outside to read it, saying that I must not let anyone see its contents. It was a very short note, and ran as follows ".

Since your intuition
led you in the right direction & made you understand
that it was my desire you
should go to Adyar im-
mediately — I may say
more. The sooner you
go the better. Do not lose
one day more than you
can help. Sail on the
5th if possible Join
Upasika at Alexan-
dria. Let no one know
you are going and
may the blessing of

our Lord, and my
poor blessing sh
I shield you from Eve-
ry Evil in your
new life.
Greeting to you
my new chela

K H.

Show my notes
to no one.

THE SECOND LETTER FROM THE MASTER K. H.

Since your intuition led you in the right direction and made you understand that it was <u>my desire</u> you should go to Adyar <u>immediately,</u> I may say more. The sooner you go the better. Do not lose one day more than you can help. Sail on the 5th if possible. Join Upasika at Alexandria. Let no one know you are going and may the blessing of our Lord, and my poor blessing shield you from every evil in your new life.

Greeting to you <u>my new chela</u>.

K. H.

Show my notes to no one.

THE SECOND LETTER OF THE MASTER

Before I comment on the second letter, let me deal first with the sacrifices which Mr. Leadbeater made when he decided to follow his Master. For there were sacrifices, and knowing about them may clear the vision of some from whom also sacrifices will be demanded, when their time comes to follow their Master.

The first sacrifice was a complete break with his family. To leave suddenly all near relations—especially those who had helped him in his career—without a particle of reason, meant of course never to hope to be received back into their circle again. We can imagine the utter astonishment of the dignified cleric, his uncle, at his nephew's declaration that in three days' time he was severing his connexion with the parish, leaving it seriously handicapped in its regular routine. And this for no more evident reason than that of a man whose mind had become unhinged through Spiritualism, Theosophy and similar unholy allurements.

Nephew and uncle and aunt never met again, even after Mr. Leadbeater returned to England five years later. He did once meet another aunt who was very fond of him ; and once a cousin or two. But for all practical purposes, though he was of an old family [1] and in the " County set ", he was outside their pale, as a renegade and wastrel who had thrown away his opportunities.

The second sacrifice was the renunciation of all his worldly prospects. It is true that he was only a curate, but he had certain unusual abilities to " get people together ", and make them work as a united band for a noble cause. His ability as an organizer—as

---

[1] The Leadbeater family was Norman French in origin, with name Le Bâtre (the builder), later Englished to Leadbeater. The senior branch of the family settled in Northumberland, whence a junior branch established itself in Ireland. Some facts about this junior branch are given in the two volumes of *The Leadbeater Papers*. The senior branch followed the fortunes of " Prince Charlie " of the Stuart dynasty and became Jacobites ; from that day—though they became loyal subjects later of the English Crown—it was the custom of the family to christen the eldest son Charles.

choirmaster, Sunday School director, and creator of boys' and girls' clubs ; his love of athletics—he was good at tennis, a fine swimmer, and could do something at cricket too ; above all, the capacity he had to inspire boys and girls " to live pure, speak true, right wrong, follow the King "—all these went to make him not merely a priest, but just that type of priest whom the Church of England wanted. I give as an appendix an account of this aspect of Mr. Leadbeater by the late James W. Matley who was a boy in Bramshott Parish, and later and to his dying day a devoted friend and admirer of his " elder brother ".

Mr. Leadbeater furthermore had a deep devotion to the Church of England. He was an enthusiast of the beauty and history of its Cathedrals, its music and hymns (even to the last he knew many hymns and tunes by heart). As a " High Church tory ", the Church of England was to him the very root of all that was great in the English cultural heritage, and for him in the greatness of that Church lay the greatness of England, though he had very little leaning to Theology. It is to such a type of young priest of the Church of England that his pathway lies to rectories or vicarages, deanships and canonries, and so to a bishopric.

It was this same ability of gathering round him a band of young and old to work devotedly for a common cause which he carried into his activities as a Theosophist—in Ceylon as an organizer of Buddhist vernacular and English schools, Sunday Schools and Wesak carol parties ; in England and the United States in Lotus Circles and Round Tables ; at Adyar gathering round him a band of secretaries, writers of letters and articles, and budding Theosophical lecturers and authors, watchful that each should be led to find his niche in the common edifice of work ; in Australia, welding young and old into one solid phalanx to work together unselfishly and *hard* in the various causes dear to the Masters.

Lastly, there was one sacrifice which Mr. Leadbeater made, to which he rarely alluded. Once when speaking to me of his coming out to India, he mentioned the incident, but quite casually, as if it were all a part of " the day's work." It was the sacrifice of all of a young man's plans of happiness in marriage to the girl of his dreams. For he was deeply in love with a girl, whom he had known many years, the sister of his schoolboy chum. He had never let her know that he loved her, first because he was quite shy, and thought himself quite unworthy of her ; and secondly he did not wish to stand in her way in preferring someone else to him, for as he said to me : " A fellow can't ask a girl to marry him on £120 a year "—which was his salary as a curate. But he had strong hopes of preferment, and looked forward to the time soon when he could offer marriage to her.

As mentioned already, his uncle had a good deal of influence. The Rev. Mr. Capes's College, Queen's, had several " livings " in its gift ; Bramshott Parish itself was such a " living ". Mr. Leadbeater's period as a curate, with the abilities which he showed in the management of a parish, and with good looks on his side, was the first step in a fairly sure career.

When, however, Mr. Leadbeater read the Master's letter, even love itself was renounced instantly with all other things to follow him. In after years he used to remark with a little pride that he had lived up to the motto of his family coat-of-arms, " Toujours prêt "—" Always ready ". Perhaps it was the lesson which he learnt from this sacrifice which made him often say, especially when speaking to young people, " For a young man, it is often the case of Occultism—or marriage ". He had not the slightest aversion to marriage as a sacred and honourable institution. There are chelas of the Masters who are not celibates but married men and women. But it does sometimes happen to a young man or young woman who is " on the fringe " of chelaship, or even at a later stage, that his or her character does not know how to play rightly the dual rôles both as a server of the Master and as husband or wife, or as father or mother. The cares and obligations of married life become too absorbing sometimes,, and the bright hopes of joy in sacrifice for the Cause of Humanity fade away in the distance, and the aspirant grows to be a " much married " man or woman.

Once we have made our sacrifice, and we look back on our pain, it seems almost as nothing, in the joy of the new life and light found thereby. But before and at the moment of sacrifice, it is the fact, as says, *Light on the Path :*

> " Before the soul can stand in the presence of the Masters,
> its feet must be washed in the blood of the heart."

There was a certain day for me in November 1889, when I was thirteen, when my feet were " washed in the blood of the heart." That day the Master received me as his chela. I have described what happened in the chapter, " The Master ", in my little *Christ and Buddha.*

Since your intuition led you

These opening words of the second letter show us how difficult is the path to the Master. Had Mr. Leadbeater weighed carefully the pros and cons of the situation merely with his mind, his decision would have been delayed. Undoubtedly he would sooner or later have become a chela ; but he would have lost the unique opportunity presented to him by the crisis in the Theosophical Society. H. P. B. was leaving the next morning ; he had said goodbye to her and it was unlikely, that he would meet her again for many years. But he acted in the light of that mysterious faculty dormant in us all called " Intuition ". The term used to describe it in Theosophical studies is " Buddhi ", but its meaning is different from that given to it usually in Sanskrit.

It is a characteristic of the Intuition that it acts *from the future,* and not from the past or the present ; it is excellently described by the phrase used for it by Lawrence of Arabia : " the unperceived foreknown ". It was not possible for the Master to suggest that Mr. Leadbeater's presence was urgently needed at Adyar. Mr. Leadbeater might have decided to go to Adyar in a month's time, or in two or three months, after all his affairs had been properly put in order. But his intuition grasped the Master's thought, and he decided to drop everything and leave at once.

Very noteworthy is the emphasis which the Master K. H. has laid on Intuition, as a very necessary requisite in one's character, if one is to unravel the mysteries of the Path of Occultism.

In a letter to Miss Arundale written in 1884 occur these phrases.[1]

> " the continual performance of duty under the guidance of a well-developed Intuition."

[1] *Letters from the Masters of the Wisdom,* First Series, Letter XX.

" From their ignorant and malevolent intolerance you appeal
to us, because your intuition tells you that they will not
accord you justice."

Two years later the Master wrote to Mr. Leadbeater:
" Believe in your better intuitions."[1]

Somewhat earlier, in writing to Colonel Olcott, the Master
said :

" Intuitive as you naturally are, chelaship is yet almost a
complete puzzle for you."[2]

And the whole problem was stated earlier by the Master in
the following :

" It was never the intention of the Occultists really to conceal
what they had been writing from the earnest determined
students, but rather to lock up their information for safety
sake, in a secure safe-box, the key to which is—intuition." [3]

And lastly, on this subject of the intuition, is an action
of the Master to test the intuition of a would-be-chela. In 1883 the
Master was in India, and visited Colonel Olcott twice at Lahore, not
in astral form but in his physical body. On the first occasion Colonel
Olcott was sleeping in a tent ; it was divided by a curtain, and on
the other side was a certain W. T. Brown of Glasgow, who had
arrived in India that year. After waking Colonel Olcott, the Master
left with him a letter in which are these words :

" I go now to young Mr. Brown to try his intuition."

Standing by Mr. Brown's side the Master placed a letter in
his hand ; the Master's touch awoke Mr. Brown, but so great was
his nervousness that it paralysed him, and he refused to turn his face
to the Master. Later, Mr. Brown received a long letter from the
Master of kindly advice and encouragement, but frankly telling him
that he was not ready.

" *You are not ready*, that is all. If you are earnest in your
aspirations, if you have the least spark of intuition in you,
if your education as a lawyer is complete enough to enable
you to put facts in their proper sequence and to present

---

[1] See later the *third* communication received from the Master K. H. by C. W. Leadbeater.
[2] *The Mahatma Letters to A. P. Sinnett*, Letter LXVII.
[3] *The Mahatma Letters to A. P. Sinnett*, Letter XLVIII.

your case as strongly as you in your inmost heart believe it to be, then you have material enough to appeal to any intellect capable of perceiving the continuous thread underneath the series of facts." [1]

But Mr. Brown finally failed to " make good ". Very quickly he lost interest in the Society, and it is said that in the end he joined the Roman Catholic Church.

to go to Adyar immediately

Why was the Master anxious that Mr. Leadbeater should go to Adyar " *immediately* " ? The answer to this lies in the Master's words later, " Join Upasika at Alexandria." H. P. B. was leaving for Liverpool the morning after Mr. Leadbeater received the second letter to sail to India. There were accompanying her Mr. Alfred J. Cooper-Oakley and his wife Mrs. Isabel Cooper-Oakley. Neither of these were chelas. Nothing that Mr. Cooper-Oakley did showed that he ever aspired to chelaship ; Mrs. Cooper-Oakley did, but became a chela several years later. But so far as H. P. B.'s health and affairs were concerned, neither of them were of much use. I never met Mr. Cooper-Oakley though I have heard something about him ; but I knew Mrs. Cooper-Oakley well. Mr. Cooper-Oakley was a Cambridge man and so presumably scholarly ; but he was introspective and given to fits of deep depression and gloom. Though he went to India with H. P. B., and stayed at Adyar for some years as assistant to Colonel Olcott, he was tepid in his devotion to Theosophy. He left Adyar to become the Registrar of the University of Madras, and was found one morning dead in bed, due to an overdose of a narcotic. There is nothing on record to show that he ever felt any personal attachment to H. P. B.

His wife did ; she was utterly devoted to H. P. B. But she was constantly worried by want of health, and required much attention. When she reached India, she found that her health suffered more than she expected, and she was forced to return to England. In spite of various and continued handicaps to health, Mrs. Cooper-Oakley toiled day after day to the end of her life to serve the Masters

---

[1] *Letters from the Masters of the Wisdom*, First Series, Letter XXII.

and the Theosophical Society. In her devotion to them and H. P. B. she was flawless. But neither she nor her husband could be called upon for strenuous service.

There was however one valuable quality in Mr. Leadbeater ; he was *dependable*. This H. P. B. knew ; otherwise she would not have written with her own hand, at the bottom of an article of his in *The Theosophist*, August, 1886, " a brave heart "[1], nor called him in the copy of her *Voice of the Silence* which she gave him, " my sincerely appreciated and beloved Brother and friend."[1] He reverenced H. P. B. as the mouthpiece of the Masters, but also admired her for herself, and was her loyal servant. Colonel Olcott was far away at Adyar ; H. P. B. started on her long journey to India with only the two Cooper-Oakleys. It was the Master's great desire that H. P. B. should have at her side a man who was a *man*.

In addition to this, Adyar was in the greatest need of capable assistants to help Colonel Olcott in what appeared to be a critical and overwhelming situation. Damodar K. Mavalankar was there, selfless, pure, and heart, brain and soul dedicated to the Master. But he felt crushed under his burden, and early in 1885 his Master acceded to his prayer to be released, and he was called to Tibet to be with his Master. Dr. Franz Hartmann was at Adyar, but he was not a chela, and he was hostile to Damodar. Though the two Masters M. and K. H. had several Hindu chelas in India, very few could be released from their work to come to Adyar, nor had they just the capacity needed to help Colonel Olcott and H. P. B. in that particular crisis.

Perhaps the Master counted on one further value that Mr. Leadbeater had in the crisis. That a clergyman of the Church of England should come out to India with H. P. B., when she was proclaimed a trickster by the missionaries, and openly attest as he did not only faith in the Masters and in her, but also his conviction of the greatness of Oriental religions (Mr. Leadbeater accepted Buddhism when the party came to Ceylon), all these things did have an effect on the mind of the public in Ceylon and India, and held many steady who were wavering.

[1] See later for the photographic reproduction.

Sail on the 5th

It may seem strange to those who do not know what the Adepts really are that the Master, though living in Tibet, should know what are the steamship routes to India and the possibilities of travel. Mr. Leadbeater received the second letter during the early hours of the morning of November 1st, as I find an entry in his diary : " Back to Sinnett's at 2 a.m. with latch-key ". That same morning H. P. B. and the two Cooper-Oakleys left for Liverpool, to sail from there to Port Said, where they were to transfer to a steamer to Madras. " Join Upasika at Alexandria ", instructed the Master. If Mr. Leadbeater could not join her in Egypt, much that the Master had planned could not be achieved. Mr. Leadbeater now takes up the story.

> " Madame Blavatsky left London later on in the same day for Liverpool, where she boarded the S. S. *Clan Drummond.* Meantime I was bustling round to steamer offices trying to obtain a passage for myself. The P. and O. steamer which was to leave on the 5th had absolutely not a berth vacant in any class, so I was reluctantly compelled to seek else-where ".[1]

By the month of October all berths on vessels to India have been booked long ahead ; it is the beginning of the rush from England of the " cold season " visitors to India. There were not so many steamship lines to India fifty-seven years ago as now. The only way to carry out the instructions of the Master was to go over-land to Marseilles and hope to get to Alexandria on some French steamer. Mr. Leadbeater found that this could be done, provided he left London on the night of the 4th at latest.

This was what he did. But we see from the brief entries in his diary what a task it was. For he had to uproot himself completely from his English life and home and " burn his boats behind him." He had a fair library, and the most needed books had to be packed to be sent after him ; he had a telescope and this too had to be packed carefully and arranged to be shipped to Madras. How he managed to get his tropical outfit in time I do not know, for

---

[1] *How Theosophy came to me,* p. 64.

London then did not have the dozens of " colonial outfitters " there are to-day. The following brief entries in the diary tell a vivid tale.

1st November. In London buying outfit. Down [to Liphook] by 4.10 train. Up late with F. and J.[1]

2nd November. Last [Sunday] at Bramshott. Up till 3 a.m. with F. and J.

3rd November. Hard at work all day [with] final arrangements. Firework display. Up till 3 a.m. with F. and J.

4th November. Buying goods and settling accounts. To town by 8.16 a.m. train. Left 9.5 p.m. from Charing Cross. Mohini[2] and Miss A.[3] saw me off. Very stormy crossing the Channel.

In his reminiscences, *How Theosophy came to me*, Mr. Leadbeater remarks :

" I hurried down to pack my goods and chattels and to make my final arrangements ; and I may say that I did not go to bed until I had left England."[4]

I believe one of the " final arrangements " was to arrange for certain payments on behalf of young Jim Matley, so that he could be entered as a cadet in the Mercantile Marine in one of the principal lines, for the boy's parents were not well off, and were unable to help their younger son to realise his dreams of becoming a sailor.

Reaching Paris at 6 a.m. on the 5th, Mr. Leadbeater left for Marseilles at 11.15 the same morning, and reached Marseilles at 6 the next morning, and went on board the French Steamer for Alexandria. When, however, he reached Alexandria, H. P. B. had left for Port Said. Though he was delayed five days by quarantine, he did join her after all at Port Said, before her steamer for Madras arrived.

" Madame Blavatsky's last word to me in London had been : ' See that you do not fail me ' ; and now her greeting was : ' Well, Leadbeater, so you have really come in spite of all difficulties.' I replied that of course I had come, and then when I made a promise I also made a point of keeping it ;

---

[1] Frank W. Matley and his younger brother James W. Matley.
[2] Mohini Mohun Chatterjee.
[3] Miss Francesca Arundale.
[4] p. 65.

to which she answered only, " Good for you ! ", and then plunged into an animated discussion—all discussions in which Madame Blavatsky took part were invariably animated—which had evidently been interrupted by my arrival." [1]

Mr. Leadbeater then narrates how suddenly H. P. B.'s plans were changed by order of her Master. Instead of waiting at Port Said for the steamer for Madras, the whole party went to Cairo. During the railway journey from Ismailia to Cairo, H. P. B. received a precipitated message from the Master K. H., in which there was one sentence for Mr. Leadbeater :

Tell Leadbeater that I am satisfied with his zeal and devotion.

After a few days' stay at Cairo, H. P. B. sent Mr. Leadbeater back to Port Said " as a kind of *avant courier*, to make arrangements in advance for some special comforts for Madame Blavatsky." H.P.B. and the Cooper-Oakleys joined the boat at Suez.

Let no one know you are going

This prohibition naturally did not apply to four persons, with whom Mr. Leadbeater was closely in touch, his hosts Mr. and Mrs. Sinnett, and Miss F. Arundale and Mr. Mohini Chatterjee, both chelas. It was at Miss Arundale's house at 77 Elgin Crescent that both H. P. B. and Mohini Chatterjee were staying. There were however many Theosophists round H. P. B., a few who were true Theosophists, but others that only in name, who were attracted more by occult phenomena than by the Ancient Wisdom. There was also the Kingsford-Maitland group of Theosophists who cared nothing for the Hindu-Buddhist tone in the teachings of the Masters. We can well imagine the curiosity aroused among the Theosophists had the news been circulated that letters from the Masters were again being received in London, in spite of the so-called " Coulomb exposure." The members of the London Lodge knew Mr. Leadbeater ; a member in clerical dress was a rarity among Theosophists. If they knew he was going to Adyar, no doubt a farewell meeting would have

---

[1] *How Theosophy came to me*, p. 68.

been arranged—as among Theosophists today. Wherein lay the harm should all know that he was going to India ?

We know from the letters of the two Masters, M. and K. H., that their action in initiating the Theosophical Movement was challenged by those " dark powers ", called Dugpas in Tibet, who are ever on the watch to hinder the progress of Humanity. The true originators of the Madras attack on the Society were not the Coulombs or the Madras missionaries, but these dark powers who used them (of course unknown to themselves) as cat's-paws and agents. In this struggle between the Adepts and their enemies, these dark powers are ever trying to tempt, entrap and lead astray every one known to be a chela. Undoubtedly Mr. Leadbeater would have to meet their attack sooner or later. But the Master, in this time of strain and danger, did not desire at the moment that additional complication.

When the second letter was received, no one except Mr. Leadbeater himself and H. P. B. knew that he had become a chela—not even his friend Mr. Sinnett. Had many known and talked of it, enough thought-currents and clouds regarding the matter would have been set in motion to draw the attention of the dark powers to Mr. Leadbeater and to the rôle he was going to play as a helper of H. P. B. They would try hard to upset the Master's plan ; it was quite possible that they could arrange for an accident or some *contretemps* so that Mr. Leadbeater should miss his train and steamer connexions, and so not join H. P. B. in Egypt. It is a general rule in Occultism, " the less said the better," when carrying out a plan.

May the blessing of our Lord

In the first letter, the Master invoked " our Lord's the Tathâgata's *memory* ". On accepting Mr. Leadbeater as a chela the Master now invokes " the *blessing* of our Lord ", of the Tathàgata.

The Adepts do not use words in a slipshod way, as is constantly our custom in our common speech. The word " blessing " today has lost its pristine significance, and in a phrase like " your father sends you his blessing ", little more is understood than a wish of goodwill and affection.   But there is something far more than that in a *real* blessing.

A blessing is a *power* transferred by him who blesses to him who is blessed, an energy which is incorporated into the receiver's nature to purify and strengthen him. Every one of us has such a power which we can pass on to another. It is evident that the amount, quality and intensity of that power depends upon the stage in spirituality and evolution of the giver of the blessing.

More wonderful is the fact that the more blessings we give the more the power to bless increases in us. For what we give to another with our soul—the only true blessing—is not ours ; we are, as we give, the channel of a greater Giver, for " every good gift and every perfect gift is from above, and cometh down from the ·Father of Lights, with whom is no variableness, neither shadow of turning." In this process of conveying "from above," there are stages, just as there are " steps " when an electric current of tens of thousands of volts is " stepped down " to a voltage of two hundred and twenty or one hundred and ten for house usage.

The great Lord Gautama Buddha, the Tathâgata, possessed of a spiritual greatness beyond our earthly conceptions, had when on earth a Blessing to give, whose power for good we can but dimly understand. But after He " entered Nirvana " that Blessing cannot come down to earth *except through those who are linked to Him on that plane.* These souls are His disciples, who " live and move and have their being " in Him. Being such a disciple of the Lord, the Master K. H. has the privilege of giving " the Blessing of the Lord ", that is to say, of charging the recipient with the Lord's Blessing. He uses this power as he says to Mr. Leadbeater, " May the blessing of our Lord shield you from every evil in your new life."

and my poor blessing

One might well ask why the Master should use this very depreciatory phrase about himself. Yet that very use leads us to a great fact of the Occult Hierarchy which has a deep significance. Not once but all the time consistently, the Adepts show a wonderful reverence towards Him who was the last Buddha of Humanity,

Gautama Buddha. For He was the first of our Humanity to achieve, through His love and self-sacrifice for our sakes, the height of development as a Buddha of Humanity.

In the arrangements for the guidance of Humanity in what is termed the Occult Hierarchy, the three greatest Adepts form a Triangle of the forces of the Solar Logos. They are the Lord of the World, the Buddha, and the Mahachohan, each being an embodiment to the world of the power and the nature of the First Logos, Second Logos and the Third Logos respectively. On each globe of the seven Rounds of our Earth Chain, such a Triangle directs the operation of the evolutionary forces on that globe. During the period when the Life Wave manifests on a globe, there are three Lords of the World, seven Buddhas, and of Mahachohans a number which has not been revealed.

During the long past of Humanity, in the first three Rounds and up to the period of the Fourth Race of the Fourth Round, the office of Buddha has been held by Adepts who have come to the Earth Chain from other evolutionary systems more advanced than ours, like Venus. But it was the Lord Gautama Buddha who was the first of our Humanity to achieve the level of Buddhahood. Buddhist books narrate His action of will and renunciation, and the Adepts confirm the Buddhist legend as in the main correct in substance. I have narrated that legend in a tale for children.[1]

The Resolve

" Long, long ago there lived on earth a noble and brave man, by name Sumédha. In those days there moved among men a Wonderful Being, a Buddha. He was called the Buddha Dîpankara. One day the Buddha and His saints were coming to a certain city. The people of the city were joyful at His coming, and everything was done to make the city beautiful. The roads were swept and sprinkled, the trees hung with flags, and everything was made to look brave. Sumédha joined in this work, for he, too, knew what a glorious person a Buddha is, and wanted to show

[1] *Christ and Buddha.*

his reverence. Sumédha had a part of the road to level, and sweep, and decorate ; but when the Buddha came, his work was not all done, and there was one big puddle in the middle of the road, that the Buddha would have to go through. Sumédha would not permit such a thing, and so he lay face down in the mud, so that the Buddha might walk over his body to the other side. And as he thus lay down he said to himself : ' May I some day be a Buddha like Buddha Dîpankara ; may I, also, some day save the world.'

" The Buddha walked over his body, and then stopped, and looked at Sumédha on the ground. Then He looked far into the future with the vision of a Buddha, and saw that, ages thence, Sumédha would have his aspirations fulfilled and would live on earth as a Buddha, the Buddha Gautama. So He spoke to Sumédha and to the others round him and said : ' This Sumédha is a future Buddha. One day he will be a Buddha, and will save the world.'

The Nomination

" After the Resolve, many, many ages passed by. Many Buddhas came and spoke their Message, each in His turn giving over to His successor the spiritual welfare of the world. But all these Buddhas were not of us. There was none then among us who could take that exalted office, and so the Buddhas came to us from far-off Venus and the Devas. But the time was coming when men should do their own work unaided, when its Buddhas and Manus should be the flowers of this our humanity. Who should be the first Buddha, the first great flower of our human tree ?

" In those days two only among the millions of men stood towering above the rest in might of grace and love— Sumédha and Another. In later days we know them as Gautama and Maitreya, Buddha and Christ. Great as They were then, yet neither was ready to qualify for the office of the Buddha-to-be, of the Fourth Root Race. If neither was ready for the office at the proper time, surely humanity would suffer. Yet it seemed almost impossible to qualify in time, so much there was to do, so little time to do it in. " Then, little Flower, for love of you and me, and millions like us, the Lord Buddha made the determination that, cost what it might, He would force His evolution, so that when the time came for a Buddha to appear to comfort men's hearts, the world might not go unaided. Life after life He toiled, undertaking a superhuman task ; so great was His renunciation, so stupendous His achievement, that even the greatest of Adepts, little Flower, speak in awe and love and reverence of the love He bore us, that made Him sacrifice Himself thus for our sakes. So of the two, on the same level of advancement long ago, One, Gautama, took the Nomination, while the Other, Maitreya, came with Him each step of the way as His chief helper.

The Consummation

" Two thousand six hundred years ago, Sumédha moved among men as a Buddha of Humanity. That birth of His was in India, and men called Him for a while Prince Siddhârtha of the Gotama clan ; but when His work was consummated, and He reached Buddhahood, He called himself Samana Gotama the Tathâgata. For eighty years He lived among men, that last of many times ; for forty-five years He preached and taught, loving His fellowmen more dearly than a mother loves her only child. To each He spoke as suited to his understanding ; to priests and scholars in deep terms of philosophy, to Chatta the little boy in boyish verses for him to sing.
" When the time came for Him, the Buddha, to pass away, He left that form, never again to return in body born of woman ; and so leaving, He gave into the hands of His successor, Maitreya, Lord of Compassion, Christ the Anointed, your welfare and mine, little Flower, and that of the other sixty thousand millions who form our humanity."

The great Adept known as the Mahachohan once said, describing Himself and His fellow-Adepts, that they were all " the devoted followers of the spirit incarnate of absolute self-sacrifice, of philanthropy, divine kindness, as of all the highest virtues attainable on this earth of sorrow, the man of men, Gautama Buddha ".[1] And later, one of the Masters speaking of their wisdom and love when compared to those of the Lord Buddha said, " We feel as if we are dust beneath His feet."

It is for this reason that the Master K.H., having given Mr. Leadbeater " the blessing of our Lord ", then gives him " my poor blessing."

Shield you from every evil

Mr. Leadbeater is no longer with us to attest in what manner the Master shielded him, from 1884, when he entered the Master's work, to 1934 when he was released from that work on the physical plane. During a close and intimate collaboration with him of forty-five years, I never noticed a single moment when his utter trust in the Master wavered by even the tiniest flicker, nor when his enthusiasm for the Master's work flagged. During the eleven years of my life with him in England, from 1889 to 1900, when he provided for me and for my education, life was not smooth. He had no means of his own, and had to earn his living first as a tutor to Mr. Sinnett's son, then as a teacher giving English lessons to foreigners in London, and later as a journalist on the staff of the London office of the *Pioneer* newspaper of India. There was a period when his income was so low, that he and I lived in a tiny room, for which seven shillings were paid for rent. It had just enough room for two beds and a table and a couple of chairs and a box or two and a wash-stand. His considerable collection of books was tied up in bundles and placed under the two beds. I had my classes to attend and he his lessons to give or his office to go to. My share was to look after our very modest housekeeping. I recall a day when the only money in hand was one half-penny, though a few shillings were expected in the evening. Fortunately he had still some good clothes left, for it was *de rigeur*

---

[1] *Letters from the Masters of the Wisdom,* Letter I.

that at the meetings of Mr. Sinnett's Lodge, the London Lodge, of which Mr. Leadbeater was secretary, all should be in full evening dress. There were occasions when his dress suit and gold watch were pledged with the pawn-broker.

In the "outer world", there were ups and downs for him ; and a particularly trying time in 1906, when his greatest colleague, Annie Besant, seemed to break the bonds of a deep friendship between them. But his attitude was one of serenity, for the only thing that mattered was that he should be true to the Master's work, and not be swayed by the judgment which others formed of him, though he felt much the estrangement from his greatest friend. But he said then with perfect confidence, " It will be all right, for presently she will understand." As to the fact that even some of his oldest and most balanced friends, on whose sanity he thought he could rely, turned against him, he was content to remember St. Paul's saying : " Who art thou that judgest another man's servant ? To his own master he standeth or falleth ". This thought is to a chela the lighthouse beacon of home when tossed in the stormy seas of karma. " To my own Master I stand or fall ; he is my judge—not any other." Such a trust in the Master is only another aspect of a trust in himself.

There was one occasion when his Master's " shield " came before him and prevented serious injury. It was a very stormy winter evening in London, and he was returning home from a lesson, with head bent down and struggling to hold his umbrella against the wind and the rain. Suddenly he heard the Master's voice, " Jump back, quick." He sprang back instantly, and he had scarcely done so when there crashed at his feet a large chimney-pot, dislodged by the wind—or by a Dugpa. When he returned home, he told me what had happened only a few minutes before.

I know myself what is the Master's " shield ", and I must give my testimony to it, though it means the drawing aside of the curtain which hides from the world one's inner life. I do so, in the trust that it may encourage others to pledge themselves again and again to be " firm to the end ". The Master has never lessened my karma, nor prevented me from making blunders. But, seeing that I was com- mitted to his work, and was trying to serve the Cause of Humanity in my little measure as he serves in his large measure, when I was in the depths, the light of his tenderness and understanding has shone before me ; and when in the sunshine, he has flashed before my imagination and idealism greater ideals still to pursue. There was an occasion in this life when the most horrible karma of all my lives, beyond the wildest dreams of my imagination, had to be endured, a block of karma which had to be got out of the way, but the violence of whose onrush would certainly have swept me off my feet to destruction. Thirty-one years before it happened he foresaw its coming, and gave me a precious gift, a true " Remember me ", a source of inspiration which was for many years a surprise to me because I had not then earned it, though I have ever had for him the wonder of a child, for the utter kindness and beauty, the wisdom and power of a father, to gaze on whom was fascination and joy. He foresaw the work I would do for him despite the defects of my character, and desired that I should slowly grow in the special resistance I needed in the trial to come. And three months before the karma commenced, when I lived in the sunshine, he showed me, with not a hint of the disaster which was to happen so soon, the picture of a future of eternal joy of which I never dreamed, *after* that karma should be done with. So, through all the years of the terrible trial, when he could not make the anguish of my pain one whit the less, the vision he gave stood before me, teaching me never to lose hope, for " Lo, I am with you always, even unto the end ", and to be utterly certain past all doubt how sunshine and joy, not for my sake but for that of others, would be mine once again. Thus has been his *shield* to me.

Were Mr. Leadbeater with us at this moment he would say to all as I am saying, " Trust in thy Master ; work tirelessly for him ; and he shall give thee thy heart's desire ".

Greeting to you, my new chela.

The aspiration of lives was thus fulfilled. For Mr. Leadbeater had known the Master K. H. in many previous incarnations, and tried to follow him. But it was only this life that his karma brought him to the gateway of the Path to Liberation, which is also the Path of Joy in Service. The " memory of our Lord the Tathâgata " flashed out in the Ego, and the personality leapt into what seemed to the lower mind the dark of an utter unknown. The intuition shone at a great crisis, and into the space of twelve hours were condensed the experience and the work which were said to require on the average seven years.

Show my notes to no one.

They were shown to me, with the Master's sanction, years afterwards. But it was only in 1908 that, with the Master's permission, the letter was published in *The Theosophist* of January of that year.

When the letter was then published, Mr. Leadbeater purposely left out this postscript, "Show my notes to no one". And similarly, I left it out when in 1919 I reprinted the letter in *Letters from the Masters of the Wisdom*, First Series. Why ?

The explanation which I have to give is the most difficult part to write of this commentary on these letters of the Master K. H. For it deals with the deep disappointment which a great Theosophist *who loved his Master* gave to that Master, through intellectual pride and lack of intuition.

Among the stalwarts of the Theosophical Society, next to H. P. B. and Colonel Olcott, was A. P. Sinnett. A wonderful achievement was his when through his *Occult World* he announced to the Western world the existence of the Adepts and of their philosophy. Certainly years before H. P. B. had sent forth her monumental *Isis Unveiled* ; she and Colonel Olcott with others had in 1875 founded the Theosophical Society ; and in 1878 a brilliant work was begun in founding *The Theosophist*. But it was Mr. Sinnett who for the first time in his *Esoteric Buddhism* gave the modern world an outline of the Wisdom of the Masters, especially as to their action in the evolution of humanity. Out of the answers to multifarious questions, often on very disjointed topics, Mr. Sinnett grasped with his mind the general lines of what the Masters had to say on man, the invisible worlds, life after death, and the progress of mankind as a whole through aeons of time. With *Esoteric Buddhism* was born another presentation of the Wisdom, which clear-thinking minds of the modern world could examine and grasp.

Yet Mr. Sinnett had a strange defect. Though he had a deep love for the Master K. H., whom he addressed as "guardian", his will was deficient to change certain aspects of his character as the Master desired. To the last he had also an ingrained prejudice as to the superiority of Western races and the inferiority of Eastern races. Though he was awed sometimes by the power which the Adepts evidently possessed, he was never convinced that they, being Orientals, had really a better knowledge than he on all matters, especially as to the West. We have only to read the long correspondence between him and the Masters to note how constantly he pressed forward his views against those of the Masters, as to how Theosophy should be proved to Western minds. It was not merely in joke 'that H. P. B. in her copy of *Isis* which she gave him wrote " To the Boss," nor after naming her own Master (never with the least sense of irreverence but strictly literal in her Americanism) " the Boss ", she termed Mr. Sinnett " Sub-Boss."

It was this intellectual pride which led him to be unjust often, and even as the Master says " cruel," to both H. P. B. and Colonel Olcott. The American democratic, and (to Mr. Sinnett) the lack of polish and of " society manners " of Colonel Olcott grated on him intensely. And also to him, in most things H. P. B. was constantly in the wrong.

Little by little he grew so unreasonable in his demands on the Masters, and so unwilling to accept that there were rigid rules in Occultism that, do what the Master K. H. could, Mr. Sinnett began to erect an ever-growing barrier between himself and the " guardian " whom he loved in his heart of hearts. At last, when in 1884, after the Coulomb attack began, and his attitude to H. P. B. was one of constant blame for stupidities and blunders of which he held her guilty, the Master told him :

" Well—she is virtually dead ; and it is yourself—pardon me this one more truth—who have killed the rude but faithful agent, one moreover who was really devoted to you personally.

" Friend, beware of Pride and Egoism, two of the worst snares for the feet of him who aspires to climb the high paths of

Knowledge and Spirituality. You have opened a joint of your armour for the Dugpas—do not complain if they have found it and wounded you there." [1]

Mr. Sinnett received this letter in London on October 10, 1884, three weeks before Mr. Leadbeater received his. Earlier in July of that year, the Master wrote to Mr. Sinnett:

"I am determined to make one more effort (the last I am permitted) to open your inner intuition . . . .

"Unfortunately, however great your purely *human* intellect, your spiritual intuitions are dim and hazy, having been never developed. [2]

It must have been after October 10, and before October 31 (the date of the first letter to Mr. Leadbeater), that with some more than usual injustice towards H. P. B. Mr. Sinnett closed (all unwittingly, and therein lies his tragedy) the door in the Master's face. And so the Master wrote:

"The right is on *her* side. Your accusations are extremely unjust, and coming from *you* pain me the more. If after this distinct statement you still maintain the same attitude I shall have to express my deep regret at this new failure of ours—and wish you with all my heart better success with more worthy teachers. She certainly lacks charity, but indeed, you lack—discrimination.

Regretfully yours
K. H."

But Mr. Sinnett still maintained the same attitude, *to the end*. One year before he died, when I saw him, he was still full of his grievances, and depreciatory of H. P. B. and especially of her contribution to Theosophy. [3]

When I went to England as a boy, I lived in his house for two years. Though he was polite to me, we were mere acquaintances. He was however always cordial with Mr. Leadbeater. Yet I had much opportunity to observe Mr. Sinnett and his ways, for

---

[1] *The Mahatma Letters to A. P. Sinnett*, Letter LXVI.

[2] *The Mahatma Letters to A. P. Sinnett*, Letter LXII.

[3] But in contrast, Mrs. Patience Sinnett, a highly intellectual woman, understood H. P. B., and made allowances for her unconventional manners and impetuosity, for she loved H. P. B. And H. P. B. knew it, as did also the Masters.

in 1894 I was admitted into the Inner Group of the London Lodge as a chela of the Master, and was present at the intimate and informal gatherings of the Group which were held on most Sunday mornings in Mr. Sinnett's library for discussion.

Mr. Sinnett, even in 1889, when I joined his household, never realized that he had broken his link with the Master. Though he received no more letters, he was thoroughly convinced that the Master still communicated with him, through a lady, a clairvoyante, whom he used to put weekly into a trance, whenever she stayed with his wife and himself (for this lady, who lived in Ireland, came to London only once or twice a year). When a few years later, this lady could no longer act as the Master's mouthpiece (so Mr. Sinnett firmly believed), he sought another, and later another. And when I saw him last, the latest medium was a man. And Mr. Sinnett never doubted the genuineness of these communications received through these channels.

There was in Mr. Sinnett a strong belief, which it was the business of none of us to challenge, that if ever the Master determined to communicate, he would do so with him first, and only through him to others. It would have come distinctly as a shock to him that Mr. Leadbeater, so junior to him in all Theosophical matters, had received letters, and not he, Mr. Sinnett. The Master desired that Mr. Sinnett should not feel hurt ; and hence the words, " Show my notes to no one." So long as Mr. Sinnett lived, neither Mr. Leadbeater nor I wanted him, should he read this second letter when published, to feel hurt at this ban from the Master.

The Master knew this characteristic of Mr. Sinnett—his belief that he was the only true representative of the Master's wishes—for in a long letter which Colonel Olcott received from the Master on board ship when nearing Brindisi in 1888 (Letter XIX, *Letters from the Masters of the Wisdom*, First Series), giving him advice and instruction regarding a troublesome situation in London, the Master adds the postscript :

> " Prepare, however, to have the authenticity of the present denied in certain quarters."

That the Master was right, and what were the " certain quarters ", we see from letters written by Mr. Sinnett on October 12 and 23, 1888 to Mr. Leadbeater who was then working in Ceylon.

" One queer thing : Olcott has got with him a letter apparently from the Master K. H. received while he was on his voyage home. After making rather a mystery of it at first he ultimately showed it to me—and I do not feel at all sure of it. It reads to me very much *en suite* with the other letters in blue handwriting that came during the 1884 crisis,—when Mme. B. herself admitted to me afterwards that during that time the Masters had stood aside and left everything to various chelas including freedom to use the blue handwriting. Of course this paragraph is most strictly private to yourself. I do not want to raise a fresh storm by impugning the authenticity of the letter—which moreover has no direct reference to me—tho' it reads as tho' in a certain sense written *at* me, again a circumstance which makes it suspicious under the circs., as I know in my own heart that my inner loyalty to the Master and his ideas as far as I can interpret them is as unchangeably perfect as ever, as sound as yours and I can't say more. The letter is all just glorification of Mme.B. Well : if He made me know that He wanted me to beg Mme. B.'s pardon for having (been ?)[1] ill-judged (by) her I would go and apologise most humbly, but meanwhile I can only follow the inner Light."

" Of course Olcott in his simple guileless way takes the letter as entirely genuine without a thought of questioning it and *he* is not to be blamed for doing so . . . I have not thought it of the least use to tell Olcott that I do not believe in the authenticity of the letter."

So I conclude this pathetic story of a splendid worker for Theosophy, who might have become a far greater server still, had he had less pride of mind as also less pride of race. Of his betrayal (unconscious again) of the trust placed in him by express command by the Master *never* to publish certain personal and intimate letters of the Master and of his brother, the Master M., I say nothing here. For, a man with a perpetual grievance warps his mind, and is not fully responsible for the derelictions of duty which honour forbids.

---

[1] This word in brackets with an interrogation, and the second word following, also in brackets, are in the original.

THE THIRD MESSAGE OF THE MASTER K. H.

THE third communication from the Master to Mr. Leadbeater is not a letter, but a brief message in six lines, in blue pencil handwriting, precipitated on the last page of a letter of H. P. B. while it was passing through the post. There are several instances of this method adopted by the Masters when, instead of writing a letter, they have given its substance in interspersed words or phrases, or written across the letter.

H. P. B.'s letter, posted in Elberfeld, Germany, to Mr. Leadbeater then living in Colombo, Ceylon, deals with the tragic instance of one more failure of a chela on probation. This was a young Brahmin of South India, by name S. Krishnamachari. He was of small stature and a clerk in the Collector's office at Nellore, but between 1880 and 1881 he resigned and went to Bombay to H. P. B. and Colonel Olcott. He then dropped his name and called himself Bawajee. H. P. B. received instructions from the Masters to use Bawajee as a worker, and he was made an assistant to Damodar K. Mavalankar.

There was at this time an *accepted* chela of the Master K. H. whose name was Gwala K. Deb. I think he was a Tibetan, as for several years he had lived in Tibet with the Master. In India he was also known under an Indian name, Dharbagiri Nath. An occasion arose when the Master K. H. needed two messengers to go to Mr. A. P. Sinnett at Simla. One messenger selected was R. Keshava Pillai of Nellore, and Letters 65 and 66 in *The Masters of the Wisdom* (Second Series), detail the help which he was to give to the principal messenger, Deb.

But Deb could not go in his own physical body, as it is was being prepared for a certain occult work, which would have been made impossible if that body were to be contaminated by the coarse magnetism of the world's surroundings. Bawajee was asked, and he consented, to give up his physical body on certain occasions, so that Deb could live in it and do the work required. While Deb occupied Bawajee's body, Bawajee lived in the astral, aware that Deb was using his physical vehicle.

The task performed, Deb left, and Bawajee came back again. From this time, H. P. B., Colonel Olcott, Damodar and a few others who knew what had happened called Bawajee also Dharbagiri Nath (which was Deb's name).

When in February 1885 H. P. B. left for Europe, she was accompanied by Dr. F. Hartmann, Miss Mary Flynn and Bawajee. In 1886, when H. P. B. was living in Elberfeld in Germany, Bawajee, who had till then looked on H. P. B. with reverence, changed. H. P. B. describes the change in her letter to Mr. Leadbeater ; there are several letters of hers to Mr. Sinnett and others, which all describe this change in Bawajee, and especially one important fact, that Bawajee claimed that he was an *accepted* chela and had been with the Master in Tibet. But it was *Deb* who was the accepted chela, not Bawajee, who was only in the earlier stage of a chela on probation. Bawajee, whose body had certainly been occupied by Deb on his special mission, began on the strength of this fact to make a nucleus round him in opposition to H. P. B. In addition, he twisted facts to suit his vanity.

As a result of all this treachery and double-dealing, Bawajee was a failure. The Master says, " The little man has failed." The Master's comment on the situation is written across the last page of H. P. B.'s letter, precipitated on it during transit in the post. About a year later, Bawajee returned to India ; nothing more was heard of him in Theosophical circles. A few years later he died in obscurity.

H. P. B.'s letter also reveals the fact that, as in 1884, Mr. Leadbeater desired to send a letter to his Master, this time through H. P. B. She refused the commission, as the Masters at her request had exempted her from being their pivot on the physical plane for phenomena, after the missionary attack began, as even some who seemed to trust her began to be suspicious. It was then that Mrs. Laura C. Holloway was tried if she could be trained to be sensitive enough in the right way to serve the purpose of a pivot ; but she was a failure.   Mohini M. Chatterjee, who was already an accepted chela, was also tried, but he too failed.

H. P. B. therefore says that she returns to Mr. Leadbeater his letter to the Master.   But when H. P. B.'s letter arrived in Colombo, the letter to the Master returned by H. P. B. was not inside.   But instead, there was a message from the Master across the last page of her letter.

Elberfeld June 23/86

My dearest Leadbeater,

I was glad — sincerely — to receive your welcome letter. As to the enclosure I really do not take upon myself to send it. I cannot do it, my dear friend; I swore not to deliver any more letters & Master has given me the right & privilege to refuse it. So that I have put it aside & send it to you back as I received it. If Mohatma KH had accepted or wanted to read the letter he would have taken it away from my box, & it remaining in its place shows to me that he refuses it.

Now learn new developments. Hower is entirely against us & bent on the ruin of the T.S. A month ago he was in London & ready to sail back to India. Now, he is here — heaven knows when he will go away for he lives with Frank Gebhard (the elder son who sides with him & whom he has entirely psychologized) & he has sown dissention & strife in the Gebhard family, the mother, father, & two sons Arthur & Rudolph remaining true to the teachings of Master & me & Frank siding with him. He never comes to us

though he lives over the way — & he writes & writes
volumes of teaching against our doctrines.
He does more: he declared to all that he was
going to publish a manifesto in which
he will express regret at having contributed for five to bamboozle the public as
to the character of the Masters & what
They would & can do. He maintains that
he was for five years under maya,
a psychological illusion. He firmly believed
during that time that all the phenomena
were produced by the Masters, that he
himself was in direct communication
with Them, & received letters & orders.
etc; but now he (Mohini) knows better.
Since he came to Europe he has learned
the truth having been illuminated (!.!!)
He learnt that the Masters could never, in
no case communicate with us, not even
with their chelas; They could never write
themselves or even cause to be precipitated
ever letters or notes, by their chelas.
All such were the production of maya,
Elementals, spooks when not "frauds"
he says. " Esoteric Buddhism " is all non
sense & hallucination nothing what
is given out in the Theosophist is true.

My "Isis" & even the _Secret Doctrine_ may
hesaid have been dictated to me by some
occultist or "Spirit" — never by Masters.
When asked how is it that he comes with me
to Europe on an _order from his Master_
as he said — he now declares coolly that
he was _mistaken_; he has "changed his
mind" & knows now it was an illusion
of his own. Olcott has never, never _said_
healed any one with mesmerism, never
was helped by Masters. et cet i.

Moreover, he has slandered persis=
=tently Subba Row, Damodar, Olcott
& every one at Adyar. He made many
Europeans lose confidence in them.
Subba Row, he says, never said a truth
in his life to a European; he bamboozles
them _always_. & is a liar; Damodar
is a great liar also; he alone (Bowaji)
knows the Masters, & what they are
In short, he makes of our Mahatmas
inaccessible, _impersonal_ Beings, so far
away that no one can reach them…!!!
At the same time he contradicts himself:
to one he says he was 10 y. with chohan
K H; to another 3 years, again he went out

several times to Tibet & saw the Master only from afar when he entered & came out of the temple. He lies most awfully. The truth is that he (B.) has never been to Tibet & has never seen his Master 100 miles off. Now, I have the assurance of it from my Master Himself. He was a chela on probation, when he came to Bombay to the Headquarters, your Master ordered me to tell all. He accepted Krishna Swami; & had sent him to live with us & work for the T.S. He was sent to Simla to Mr S. that is to say, he gave up his personality to a real chela, Harbajin Nath, & assumed his name since then. As I was under pledge of silence I could not contradict him when I heard him bragging that he now lived with his Master in Tibet & was an accepted regular chela. But now when, he failed as a "probationary" owing to personal ambition, jealousy of Mohini & as suddenly developed rage & envy even to hatred of Colonel & myself — now

Master ordered me to say the truth. What do you think he did? Why, he looked me in the face & asked me what I knew of his past life! That certainly had not go to Master during the five years he was with me but that he knew Mahatma M & 62 years before he had heard of the T.S. !!! When I showed him Master's writing in which your Mahatma corroborated my statement & affirmed that he (Hodgson) had never seen him or go to Tibet — Mr B. coolly said it was a spook letter, for the Mahatma would neither write letters, nor would he ever say anything about his chelas.

Thus he hides himself behind a triple armour of non responsibility — yet is impossible to catch him for him, who, like Frank Gebhard believes that every word of B.'s is gospel. B. — denies nothing; admits everything, every phenomenon, & gets out of it by saying that it was an illusion, his "Karma" when caught in a flagrant contradiction, he gets out of it by saying that neither has any recollection of time, space or figures (!!) hence ... When shown over his ... he defended ... the doctrines of ... the Master he answers ... der an illusion ... change my mind ... is bent upon ... society ... he will ... mind ... truth ... him ... the ... expose ... he never ... lost, or will ... convulsion; ... my dear fellow don't lose courage however. The Masters are with us & will protect all those who stand firm by them. Write to Ostende poste restante to me I will be there tomorrow. Yours

H.P.B.'S LETTER TO C. W. LEADBEATER

Elberfeld, June 23/86

My dearest Leadbeater,

I was glad—sincerely—to receive your welcome letter. As to the enclosure I really do not take upon myself to send it. I cannot do it, my dear friend; I swore not to deliver any more letters and Master has given me the right and privilege to refuse it. So that I have put it aside and send it to you back as I received it. If Mahatma K H had accepted or wanted to read the letter he would have taken it away from my box, and it remaining in its place shows to me that he refuses it.

Now learn new developments. Bawajee is entirely against us and bent on the ruin of the T. S. A month ago he was in London and ready to sail back to India. Now, he is here—heaven knows when he will go away for he lives with Frank Gebhard (the elder son who sides with him and whom he has utterly psychologized) and he has sown dissension and strife in the Gebhard family, the mother, father, and two sons Arthur and Rudolph remaining true to the teachings of Masters and me and Frank siding with him. He never comes to us though he lives over the way—and he writes and writes volumes of teachings against our doctrines. He does more; he declared to all that he was going to publish a manifesto in which he will express regret at having contributed for food to bamboozle the public as to the character of the Masters and what They will and can do. He maintains that he was for five years under maya, a psychological illusion. He firmly believed during that time that all the phenomena were produced by the Masters, that he himself was in direct communication with Them, and received letters and orders, etc. ; but now he (Bawajee) knows better. Since he came to Europe he has learned the truth having been illuminated (!!!) He learned that the Masters could NEVER, in no case communicate with us, not even with their chelas; They could never write themselves or even cause to be precipitated letters or notes by Their chelas. All such were the production of Maya, Elementals, spooks, when not "frauds," he says.   "Esoteric Buddhism" is all nonsense and hallucination.   Nothing what is given out in the Theosophist is true.   My "Isis" and even the Secret Doctrine may he said have been dictated to me by some occultist or "spirits"—never by Masters.   When asked how is it that he came with me to Europe on an order from his Master as he said—he now declares cooly that he was mistaken; he has, "changed his mind" and knows now it was an illusion of his own.   Olcott has never, never healed anyone with mesmerism, never was helped by Masters, etc. etc.

Moreover, he has slandered persistently Subba Row, Damodar, Olcott and everyone at Adyar.   He made many Europeans lose confidence in them.   Subba Row, he says, never said a truth in his life to a European; he bamboozles them always and is a liar; Damodar is a great liar also; he alone (Bawajee) knows the Masters, and what They are.   In short, he makes of our Mahatmas inaccessible, impersonal Beings, so far away that no one can reach Them !!!   At the same time he contradicts himself; to one he says he was 10 y. with Mahatma K H; to another 3 years, again he went several times to Tibet and saw the Master only from afar when He entered and came out of the temple.   He lies most awfully.   The truth is that he (B.) has never been to Tibet and has never seen his Master 100 miles off.   NOW, I have the assurance of it from my Master Himself.   He was a chela on probation.   When he came to Bombay to the Headquarters, your Master ordered me to tell all He accepted Krishna Swami, and had sent him to live with us and work for the T.S.   He was sent to Simla to Mr. S. that is to say, he gave up his personality to a real chela, Dharbagiri Nath, and assumed his name since then.   As I was under pledge of silence I could not contradict him when I heard him bragging that he had lived with his Master in Tibet and was an accepted regular chela.   But now when, he failed as a "probationary" owing to personal ambition, jealousy of Mohini and a suddenly developed rage and envy even to hatred of Colonel and myself—now Master ordered me to say the truth.   What do you think he did?   Why, he looked me in the face and asked me what I knew of his past life?   That certainly he did not go to Master during the five years he was with us, but that he knew Mahatma K H 12 years before he had heard of the T.S. !!!   When I showed him Master's writing in which your Mahatma corroborated my statement and affirmed that he (Bawajee) "had never seen HIM or go to Tibet"—Mr B. cooly said it was a spook letter; for the Mahatma could neither write letters, nor would He ever say anything about his chelas.

Thus he hides himself behind a triple armour of non responsibility—and it is impossible to catch him for him, who, like Frank Gebhard believes that every word of B's is gospel. B. denies nothing ; admits everything, every phenomenon, and gets out of it by saying that it was an illusion, his Karma. When caught in a flagrant contradiction, he gets out of it by saying that no chela has any recollection of time, space, or figures (!!) hence the contradiction. When shown over his own signature that he defended phenomena and preached the doctrines of the Society and the Masters, he answers, "Oh, yes ; but I was under an illusion. Now I have CHANGED MY MIND." What can you do? He is bent upon the destruction of our Society and when he returns to India he will throw doubts into every Hindu's mind. Damodar who knows the truth about him and could expose him is far away and has no desire to return. Thus, unless Subba Row and a few earnest Hindus help Colonel to expose him (and Subbaya Chetty [1] knows he never was in Tibet) the Society is lost, or will have another tremendous convulsion. Good bye my dear fellow don't lose courage however. The Masters are with us and will protect all those who stand firm by Them. Write to Ostende, poste restante to me. I will be there tomorrow.

Your ever faithfully and fraternally,

H. P. BLAVATSKY

[Postscript at the top of the first page]

My love and blessings to Don David [2] and all the Brethren. My greatest respectful salams to the High Priest Rev. Sumangala. [3] Ask his blessing to me.

---

[1] G. Soobiah Chetty, still resident in Adyar, December, 1941.

[2] Anagarika H. Dharmapala, founder of the Mahabodhi Society.

[3] High Priest of Adam's Peak, Principal of Vidyodaya College for Buddhist Priests, a most helpful collaborator of Colonel Olcott.

THE THIRD MESSAGE OF THE MASTER K. H.

Take courage. I am pleased with you. Keep your own counsel and believe in your better intuitions. The little man has <u>failed</u> and will reap <u>his</u> reward. SILENCE meanwhile.

K. H.

THE THIRD MESSAGE OF THE MASTER K. H.

Take courage.

H. P. B. says, towards the end of her letter to Mr. Leadbeater, "Don't lose courage." All who were closely in touch with H. P. B. were aware how acutely sensitive she was to every possible detriment or danger to the Theosophical Society. After the great blow which the Society received from the attack of the missionaries, when so many failed in courage to attest openly their trust in the Society's true worth, we can well imagine how alarmed H. P. B. was at Bawajee's defection. Her anxiety certainly exaggerated his influence; because, except for the division which he created in the Gebhard family, there is no trace anywhere in the Society at the time that Bawajee's attack on H. P. B. caused any disturbance. But Mr. Leadbeater was far away in Ceylon, and H. P. B.'s letter was alarming enough for anyone to presume that one more crisis had descended on the Society.

The Master's more positive words, "Take courage," showed Mr. Leadbeater that the danger to the Society was not of the kind which rocked it to its foundations in 1884.

I am pleased with you.

Five simple words, but what life they must have brought to Mr. Leadbeater! There is none now living but I who knows what strain and discomfort were his—had he allowed himself to take note of them—at this time, when he lived in Colombo at the headquarters of the "Buddhist Theosophical Society." That Society was never "Theosophical"; and though for a while a few hundred Sinhalese became members of the Parent Theosophical Society, they were Buddhists first and last, and I doubt if more than half a dozen at most had ever an idea what Theosophy was as a philosophy or as an outlook on life. Never was the atmosphere in the Ceylon Headquarters " Theosophical ", as we understand the word.

Apart from the want of this congenial atmosphere of Adyar, the purely physical disagreeableness of the living conditions at the place, in Pettah " native town ", in one of its crowded parts, for a European of refined habits, would have made most leave it quickly. Mr. Leadbeater had, on the first floor at the end of the building abutting on a street, one small room to serve as a writing, dining and living room ; the tiny bedroom was partitioned off from the verandah by a canvas screen. He certainly had a bathroom to himself, to which he had to descend to the ground floor ; but next to it was—not a *water*-closet, for it had no water, nor even the Indian arrangement with a daily " sweeper ", but a horrible cesspool cleaned once a year. There was a printing press on the ground floor, and a meeting hall for the weekly preaching from nine at night to midnight.

The Buddhist Society made him a small allowance, and provided a servant ; but how small that " subsistence allowance " was can be gauged from the fact that he lived mostly on porridge, bread and bananas, and a little something that passed for milk. Tea and coffee were expensive luxuries. Mrs. Sinnett used periodically to send him socks and hankerchiefs.

He had to travel constantly into the villages, usually at night by bullock cart, for the day was taken up with organizing schools, and getting subscriptions and collections. The first year he travelled with Colonel Olcott, but later alone. Mr. Leadbeater's diaries for these years contain only a brief mention of the places. But what hard travel it was I realize now, having been born in the Island ; and it is only after I went to England that I realized what were the conditions he had lived in, though at the time, as born myself in such surroundings, they did not appear other than ordinary.

But he " stuck to his job." Next after Colonel Olcott, it was Mr. Leadbeater who helped to build up the Buddhist Educational Movement in Ceylon, though the Buddhists seem hardly aware of that fact, even today. Still, if the Master said, " I am pleased with you ", what mattered what others did not say ?

believe in your better intuitions

Living in Ceylon as he did, and having broken so suddenly his links with the members of the Theosophical Movement in England, there was none to keep him informed of events except the Sinnetts,[1] whose letters I have here at Adyar. Mrs. Sinnett's letters, when she reports any Theosophical event, reports but does not condemn. Mr. Sinnett felt a warm admiration for Mr. Leadbeater's purity of character and motive, and trusted him, and so speaks his mind freely. But it is nearly always with a bias against H. P. B. and Colonel Olcott. To Mr. Sinnett, nothing that Headquartes at Adyar did was the right or sensible thing ; and as to the Movement in Europe, according to his report it was barely alive, and when H. P. B. returned to London from Germany, and began to pour life again into the Society, she was doing more harm than good.

Had Mr. Leadbeater accepted as accurate all that Mr. Sinnett described, he might well be anxious for the future for the Society. For he had a profound regard for Mr. Sinnett, and it took many years before his faith in his friend as a dispassionate and reliable narrator of events lessened. Just at this period, when Mr. Sinnett's letters tended to the side of gloom, the advice to believe in his " better intuitions " was evidently necessary, since the Master gives it.

The little man has failed

How he failed is evident from H. P. B.'s letter. But *why*, who knows except the Master ? It is evident that with the privilege of being taken as a chela on probation, not only the latent good but also the latent evil came to the surface. Bawajee is one more illustration of H. P. B.'s saying, " The path of Occultism is strewn with wrecks."

and will reap his reward.

We hardly know what exactly are the karmic " rewards " which we obtain, when we fail in Occultism. Obviously, much

---

[1] Probably Miss F. Arundale wrote occasionally, but evidently nothing of importance to be kept for future reading.

depends on the causes of failure—how much of weakness, moral cowardice, pride, ambition, envy, jealousy play their part in the tragedy. Each force set in motion on the physical, astral or mental planes, whether for good or for evil, works out its result on its own plane. If the motive is good, there is nothing but good on the mental plane, a plane of far greater power than the astral or physical. Mere blunders due to heedlessness or apathy create far less evil karma than jealousy, envy and ambition.

Wherever there is a failure, great or small, one effect at least in future lives is to be met with obstacles which, one after another, bar our way, in an incomprehensible and seemingly undeserved way, when we hope eagerly to realize this or that aspiration. The "reward" of failure is frustration in future lives. Yet there is never a failure forever. And any good that has been done in the service of mankind and of the Masters (and Bawajee had a record of service for both) will bring in future lives a harvest of opportunity after opportunity, in spite of each frustration. Opportunities lost yet bring opportunities again, if somewhere in us the flame of aspiration still burns.

Silence meanwhile

Treasuring in his mind and heart what the Master said, Mr. Leadbeater kept "silent", working hard, relying on himself and, till his Master told him to give out the occult knowledge which he had gathered as a result of the Master's training, giving no indication of that occult advancement which he had made, as a chela who stood every test and was found always at his post.

LETTER OF THE MASTER K. H. TO H. S. OLCOTT

THIS is a page of the letter of the Master from which, on p. 74, I have quoted his postcript: "Prepare, however, to have the authenticity of the present denied in certain quarters."

The letter was received by Colonel Olcott in 1888, precipitated in his cabin. It is a long letter of eleven pages, and is printed as Letter XIX in *Letters from the Masters of the Wisdom*, First Series. The tenth page of the letter is the illustration which follows.

Various Theosophical workers are mentioned by their initials, among them "C. W. L."

I wish you to assure others T.T.,
R.A.M., N.K.S., N.D.C., G.K.C.,
U.U.B., T.V.C., P.V.S. N.D.C.,
C.S., C.W.L., D.N.G., D.H.,
S.N.C. Etc. among the rest, not
forgetting the other true workers
in Asia, that the stream of
Karma is ever flowing on
& we as well as they must win
our way toward Liberation. There
have been sore trials in the past,
others await you in the future.
May the faith & courage which
have supported you hitherto
Endure to the End.

    You had better not mention for
the present this letter to any one —
not even to H P B unless she speaks
to you of it herself. Time enough

LETTER OF THE MASTER K. H. TO H. S. OLCOTT

I wish you to assure others T. T., R A. M., N N. S., N. D. C., G. N. C., U. Ü. B., T. V. C., P. V. S., N. B. C., C. S., C. W. L., D. N. G., D. H., S. N. C., etc. amongst the rest, not forgetting the other true workers in Asia, that the stream of Karma is ever flowing on and we as well as they must win our way toward Liberation. There have been sore trials in the past, others await you in the future. May the faith and courage which have supported you hitherto endure to the end.

You had better not mention for the present this letter to anyone—not to even H P B unless she speaks to you of it herself. Time enough

THE INITIALS IN THE LETTER

The only names of which I feel sure are the following :

    T. T. = Tookaram Tatya

    N. N. S. = Norendro Nath Sen

    G. N. C. = Gyanendra Nath Chakravarti

    T. V. C. = T. Vijayaraghava Charlu

    P. V. S. = P. Vencata Subbiah

    C. S. = (Pandit) Chandra Sekhara

    C. W. L. = C. W. Leadbeater

    D. N. G. = Dina Nath Ganguli

    S. N. C. = S. Nilakantkumar Chatterjee.

THE ENVELOPE OF THE FIRST LETTER

THE envelope is reproduced in exact size. The address is in ink, and in the handwriting of the Master K. H.

It seems as if the Master had intended to write "England" below "Liphook," the name of the town; but as the letter was to be posted in England, he scratched out the letter "E" and wrote "Hants.", the postal contraction for Hampshire, since it is the English custom to put the name of the county when the town is not well known.

The letter, according to Mr. J. W. Matley (see Appendix I), seems to have been sent to somebody in London to post; this person in a hurry put the stamp in the wrong place and upside down. "Kensington" is a postal district in the west of London; the date is clearly "OC-30-84".

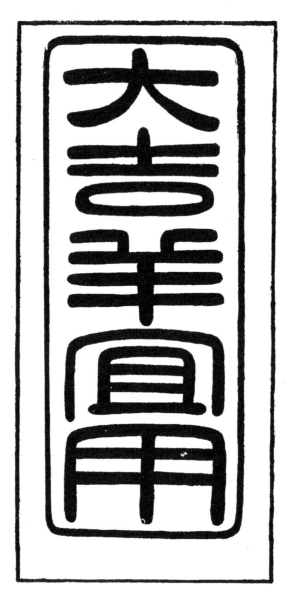

THE ENVELOPE OF THE SECOND LETTER

THE reproduction is in exact size. The envelope is of white paper, and the Chinese letters and the thick line round them are in red. The flap of the envelope is at the top. It is evidently a common envelope in use in Tibet, with a kind of "greetings card" message printed on it. Among the letters of the Masters at Adyar, there are ten envelopes of this size, in two colours, red and blue, and in several designs. The greeting on this envelope according to a Chinese gentleman is : "May great good fortune be at your service." Perhaps from among the many designs in envelopes, this particular one was chosen, as being in harmony with the benedictions at the end of the letter.

THE ENVELOPE OF H. P. B.'S LETTER

THIS is reproduced in exact size. "ELD" is the last part of the place of posting, ELBERFELD.

The German stamp on the letter has been removed for someone's stamp album.

H. P. B. ON C. W. LEADBEATER IN 1886

THE illustration below is an exact reproduction of a page of *The Theosophist*, p. 686, August 1886, in which appears an article by C. W. Leadbeater, " Anuradhapura and Mihintale ". H. P. B.'s copy of this volume of the journal is here at Adyar, and she has marked in blue pencil the last two paragraphs, as reproduced below.

The fourth and fifth temples we had not time to visit, but we were told that they were both smaller than those we saw ; one is said to contain some fine specimens of wood carving, and another gigantic reclining statue of our Lord. ✗

This account of the little that we ourselves were enabled to see cannot, of course, be considered as giving more than a mere hint of what would reward the researches of a traveller with more time at his disposal. Surely therefore when our Indian neighbours require rest and relaxation, they might do worse than pay a visit to what Mr. Burrows describes as " an artistic and archæological treat, which is perhaps unique in the East." They will at the same time be enabled to form something like a just estimate of the past history of a very interesting nation—a nation which, as the same author remarks, " could build a city of gigantic monoliths, carve a mountain into a graceful shrine, and decorate its pious monuments with delicate pillars that would have done credit to a Grecian artist."

✗ C. W. LEADBEATER.

A brave heart!

H P B

H. P. B.'S GIFT TO C. W. LEADBEATER (I)

THE following is a reproduction in exact size of H. P. B.'s words written in the copy of her *Voice of the Silence* given to C. W. Leadbeater.

To my sincerely appreciated & beloved Brother & friend W. C. Leadbeater.

H. P. Blavatsky

THE VOICE OF THE SILENCE.

H. P. B.'S GIFT TO C. W. LEADBEATER (II)

THE following is a reproduction in exact size of H. P. B.'s words written in the copy of her *Key to Theosophy* given to C. W. Leadbeater, a few months before she passed away.

To my old & well-beloved friend Charles Leadbeater. from his fraternally H P Blavatsky.

London 1891.

THE KEY TO THEOSOPHY.

CONCLUSION

WHEN that day comes when I am released from my tasks and from this prison-house of the flesh, and I return to Him " rejoicing " and bringing as my " sheaves " my record of work done " In His Name and for the love of Mankind ", I hope He will say to me, as He did to my brother, " *I am pleased with you.*"

C. Jinarājadāsa

APPENDIX I

C. W. LEADBEATER AT BRAMSHOTT PARISH

By James W. Matley [1]

C. W. L. was a curate in a parish in Hampshire called Bramshott, and lived with his mother at a cottage called " Hartford ", about a quarter of a mile from the small village of Liphook. The Rector of the parish was the Rev. W. W. Capes, an Oxford double first man ; his wife Mrs. Capes was C. W. L.'s aunt. The other curate was a Mr. Kidston who was married and lived further along the same road.

I only vaguely remember Mrs. Leadbeater ; she had such lovely white hair and a face that one took to instinctively. There was also in the parish a lay reader, an old man. When he died another curate came. Mrs. Leadbeater died before I had much to do with C. W. L., and after her death a Mr. Cartwright came as curate and shared the cottage with C. W. L. I must not forget the cat Peter, a noble tabby of great size and a favourite of C. W. L., always kept in his room night and day ; he left it with us when he went away.

In front of the cottage was a large oak tree, and on this in the winter C. W. L. would hang pieces of meat for the half-starving birds ; there was of course a nice garden of which C. W. L. was fond.

I have no idea of the date when C. W. L. came to Bramshott, in a vague way I seem to remember him always. Frank, an elder brother by six years, was first with him a great deal, and learnt to play the organ and was taught music generally, and was in the choir ; and I when old enough also came there, when about 9 years

---

[1] From 1890 till a year before his death in 1939, I used to meet " Jim Matley ", in England whenever his ship returned to England, and later when he was a planter in Papua, whenever he and I were in Australia at the same time. He wrote this account at my request several years ago. The last paragraph is from a letter received from him after Bishop Leadbeater's death.

old, I suppose. When I first seem to know C. W. L. was one Saturday ; I was with two other boys, I suppose between nine and ten years old ; we had a dog, and were going, with the aid of the dog, to catch a rabbit (I think the rabbit was fairly safe).

We met C. W. L. on the way, or rather he was with my brother on a small hill, and appeared to have been firing with a saloon pistol at some target ; he pointed the pistol towards us and fired, and for fun I dropped down ; he having seen the real thing was I fancy not greatly alarmed. The two came down to us and C. W. L. wanted to know what we were doing. We explained, and then C. W. L. told Frank that he thought it was time I was taken in hand, and that he would find for me a nicer amusement than the one I had contemplated. So there and then I was taken on, and from that time on we three were always together when possible, and became three brothers. Only studies and such like interfered with our meetings, which were at "Hartford". This was after Mrs. Leadbeater's death.

The evenings which were to spare were used in learning songs, and other music, or playing euchre ; Saturdays were used to take long walks to all the pretty places in the neighbourhood, and at times further afield to Portsmouth, seeing the sights there, and to London where at my first theatre I saw with him "Princess Ida" at the Savoy. Guildford was a favourite place, boating on the River Wey, also Midhurst and the river there. G. A. Henty's "Union Jack Field Club" was started by C. W. L. and a good few boys joined this. I think it was a club in which you promised not to be cruel to any creature, and to report anything of interest that happened amongst the creatures about you. Anyhow we at times with a crowd of boys would take walks into the Forest and across the Commons, collecting all sorts of specimens of natural history. C. W. L. of course was a favourite with boys, it was to these that he seemed to go and have most to do with.

The Church Society was also formed, this for boys and by C. W. L. In this I think we promised not to tell lies, and to be pure and good as far as in us lay. If any other boy wished to join, he had to be proposed and seconded ; then if any one had any objection on the score that he had not been truthful or had done that which was not right, he was (so to speak) black-balled for a certain time. At the meetings held every fortnight, we had songs, told stories, or had readings, also C. W. L. provided refreshment in the shape of cake, fruit and nuts ; hence there was keen competition to get into the Society, which I think was for all boys over ten. I fancy that it caused some jealousy, as of course only Church boys joined, and there was a fairly strong crowd of Dissenters there. The Juvenile Branch of the Church of England Temperance Society was also started by C. W. L., this for boys and girls, and was a success and a large number joined. This was in March 1888, and I see that I am No. 1 on the roll.

The meetings were made very attractive ; they were opened with prayer, C. W. L. having a surplice on, and a hymn or two sung, hymns that had a go in them and were enjoyed. After that the surplice was doffed, and all sorts of songs were sung, solos by any that could ; I was of use here, as I had a large stock, and the chorus was joined in by all. Readings also were read by C. W. L. or some of the boys or girls ; an annual tea was given, and also some little present I fancy, in the shape of books, decent books, too, none of that sanctimonious sort telling of impossible boys and girls ; the boys had Mayne Reid, Marryat, and Kingston ; I don't know about the girls' books.

About this time C. W. L. used to go to a good few spiritualistic séances, and one Easter we spent going to a number in London, to Mr. Husk where the famous Irresistible was, also to Eglinton. He had Husk down to " Hartford " one night for a séance ; I think that a Mr. Crowther came as well as we three. We had quite a good evening and lots of phenomena.

Astronomy was a favourite hobby of C. W. L. and he had a fine telescope ; I think that it had a 12" reflector. I know that we had many enjoyable evenings in the garden looking at stars and the moon. Once an eclipse of the moon was an event ; C. W. L. saw a shadow that was noticeable before the eclipse fairly started, and wrote to some paper as to this, and it was found to be in all probability the shadow cast by the Andes.

In the summer of 1884 we three went for a month to Ramsgate together, and had a lovely time visiting all the places near, also going across to France ; this was my first great sea trip ; I think that

C. W. L. was unwell but I was not, nor have ever been. C. W. L. taught me to swim at Ramsgate, also he nearly drowned me, and also saved me another time. We were bathing when the tide was out, and had been playing leap frog; C.W.L. tried to jump over my head into the water, but his hand slipped and his leg with a large bell mouthed pair of bathing pants slipped over my head, and we both tumbled into the water fairly deep; I don't know what happened after, but I had a bad time for a while, as I could not get clear till we were both hauled out. Another time in the sea (I had learnt to swim a few strokes) I had got to where C. W. L. was, and then tried to go on to shallow water; but the tide took us both off our feet, and myself away so far that I was nearly drowned, before C. W. L. could get to me.

He started all sorts of games for the boys, and was with them all he could be at cricket; we used to have a great deal of tennis together, and I think that he preferred this to cricket.

About this time I took up French, Trigonometry and Navigation, C. W. L. teaching me in spare time; but with meetings, choir practice and my own music lessons and the practice for that, though there was not a great deal of time, we seemed to fill it all in.

I remember C. W. L. put some music to words out of some of Mrs. Hemans' poetry. I liked the music, I don't know what special piece the words were from, they run thus, " In the shadow of the pyramid, where our brother's grave we made." I fancy that my brother Frank has the music yet.

You know from other sources that it was through Spiritualism that C. W. L. came to Theosophy. I think that he tried to reach the Master through Eglinton the spiritualistic medium. I am not quite sure now how finally he come to be a Theosophist, that is, to join the Society. Anyhow he decided to offer his services to the Master, and I think that Madame sent the message. The reply came in a curious way; a letter came to someone in England to be posted to C. W. L., and the Master had sent his message to C. W. L. in it. The man who posted the letter had of course had no idea what was in the letter.

I think that he packed up and left almost at once. There was to be a firework display on Nov. 3rd for the choir and the Church of

England Temperance members. All in both societies were invited to Hartford Cottage for a firework display, and I think there was also tea and cake. I am not sure now if the date of the firework display was for that particular day or if it was advanced. It was a great display ; we had been busy fixing on Catherine wheels and such like ready ; then we had a box of fireworks, all in nice order, so that they could be handed out as required, rockets, Roman candles, and such like. It was dark of course ; the display started about 8 p.m. A few boys were allowed to use crackers, and throw them about ; one, I forget his name, decided he would throw one into the box of fireworks. The result was simply gorgeous, and really dangerous too, every sort of firework going off at once, Roman candles shooting into the audience, and even rockets dangerously near, a wonderful display. We all decided that it was really far ahead of anything arranged. It was a hectic time ; I well remember that firework display. After the display all went home.

We three went up to Brother's[1] room to pack and sort things. Frank and I left Hartford Cottage in the early hours, Frank wheeling a wheelbarrow full of special books, to our home ; we went a short cut across fields, rough going, I was too small to use the wheelbarrow but carried things. He left on the 4th of November, 1884 ; no one but we three knew ; the rest of the folk were left in ignorance.

Written after Bishop Leadbeater's death.

His old boys have not forgotten him, and still think of all he tried to do for them, and with love I feel sure. To myself he has been all the time a Brother, and that means everything that it is possible to be I think. If it were possible, he has been more than that to me, a Brother such as the world at large has no idea of. I don't think that I can repay to him what he has done for me, only to the world at large, and I know that will please him best of all.

J. W. MATLEY

Wanganui Plantation,
Samarai, Papua.

---

[1] " Brother " was the designation by which all spoke of and addressed Bishop Leadbeater, after he settled in Sydney.

ACKNOWLEDGMENT

I DESIRE to express my thanks for quotations from *The Mahatma Letters to A. P. Sinnett*, transcribed by the late A. Trevor Barker and published by Messrs. T. Fisher Unwin.

CPSIA information can be obtained at www.ICGtesting.com
Printed in the USA
BVOW09*2356070816

458246BV00005BA/6/P

9 781161 361841